I0467905

Presentation Skills

that

Rock!

Captivating your audience in the digital era

By: Cheryl Stinchcomb

Copyright © 2014 Cheryl Stinchcomb

All rights reserved.

Legal Notice

The author has strived to be as accurate and complete as possible in the creation of this book. The contents within are accurate and up to day at the time of writing however due to the rapidly changing nature of social media and the internet some information may not be fully up to date at the time of reading.

TABLE OF CONTENTS

Introduction

The importance of learning the skill of public speaking has increased dramatically because of our digital world. The same skills taught 20+ years ago for presenting on stage are the exact same skills needed to create a marketing video, host a meeting on Skype, or live stream training through Google Hangouts on Air. Many years ago it was easy for people to avoid public speaking but with the digital world it is practically impossible. So it is critical to learn these skills and avoid being afraid of speaking in front of a group.

Out of all the things to fear in life, what do you fear most? I would expect most people to say death or afraid of heights, but speaking in front of others? Can you believe that 74% of people suffer from speech anxiety? (Resource: Statistic brain.com)

Public speaking is more than standing on stage and presenting information to a large crowd. Public speaking or presentation skills are about persuasive speech, body language, and selling your ideas to others. "Others" could be just your boss, your team, your spouse or kids, conducting a workshop, creating an instructional video for your business, hosting a live webinar or live stream training session and presenting material on the big stage as a motivational speaker.

Learning the skill set of persuasive speaking is imperative to your career or business success. I understand the importance of this skill set because being a business owner I have been on the local news, spoken at association conferences, and I market my business through online videos.

The skills that I teach in this book apply to every aspect you must achieve in your business or career. The techniques I teach will help you speak more eloquently to your boss when asking for a raise, they can help you communicate better with your loved ones, they will prepare you to present to a larger audience, and teach you how to conduct a meeting or training session through video and online live streaming.

Is public speaking scary? Yes, it can be. I remember when I first had to speak in front of a group. I was so nervous; my palms were sweating, my hands visually shaking, and my stomach tied in knots. As uncomfortable as it was, I would still rather be uncomfortable speaking in front of a group then on my death bed. Wouldn't you? [Death was the #2 fear on the top 10 list]

People are afraid to speak in front of others for many valid reasons, but I haven't found a book or training that made this learning process easy. Public speaking is a talent that can be learned, no one is born with this skill. No matter who you are, you will have to do it sometime so why not be ready to impress?

Chapter 1

Your Perception of Public Speaking

There are only two types of speakers in the world.
1. The Nervous and 2. Liars.
~Mark Twain

My First Time

Back stage the crew was moving quickly and putting props in place. Everyone is focused. Obviously the entire staff is well-trained on their job task and knows when they need to complete it. I felt like the only one that didn't know where to go and what to do. The back stage manager asked me a few questions about my Power Point presentation and then politely asked me to stand quietly to the left side of the stage behind the curtain until my queue. I was scheduled to be on stage in ten minutes. My hands began to sweat, my

stomach wanted to dry-heave, and my head kept screaming
get me out of here. I was about to go on stage in front of 1500
colleagues and conduct my first presentation on a big stage. I
have never been so frightened, but I was stuck, I couldn't
run. My name was written on the agenda; everyone was
expecting me. So I took a deep breath and slowly began to
enter the stage as they called my name, "…and here is your
Director of Training, Cheryl Stinchcomb". Thank goodness
there was a big welcome applause; at least the fear of only
two people clapping didn't come true. As I approached the
microphone I thought, "No one wants to hear what I have to
say, I am just wasting their time."

Blinded by the bright stage lights, all I could see were
merely shadows and faint silhouettes peering through the
pitch black room. If it wasn't for the noisy applause I would
have thought the company was playing a practical joke by
sending me to the wrong conference room. Before I could
open my mouth, my eyes quickly began to adjust and I could
see the first two rows of faces. The silhouettes were gone
and to my surprise my colleagues were smiling at me. I was
wrong, they didn't look bored. They looked interested. They
were eagerly waiting for me to get started. I could see it in
their eyes. Then another fearful thought crept in "What if I
forget what to say and I just stand here looking clueless?" It
was in that moment that I could see my best friend sitting on
the front row with the supporting look of *knock 'em dead, girl.*
Seeing her face gave me a boost of confidence. I didn't
forget a single word or punch line; in fact, my presentation
poured out of me with such passion and enthusiasm they
practically had to pull me off the stage. I found something

that I loved. If I would have let my negative thoughts control my actions and stop me from overcoming my fear of public speaking; I would have never learned about my hidden talent and how important learning the skill of public speaking would be to my future career success.

Tackling Your Biggest Fear

I can just say the words 'public speaking' and some people will have an immediate physical reaction. Some get a stomach ache, others may want to toss up their lunch, and certain people will go into a full blown panic attack.

> *Change the way you look at things*
> *and the things you look at change.*
> *~Wayne W. Dyer*

Yes, I have experienced a lot of anxious feelings as I was learning presentation techniques and I am also living proof that you can overcome these fears. To get past your fear and master the skill of public speaking, your perception must be changed.

At this point, you may be saying to yourself, "I don't need to get over this fear; I can avoid making speeches at any time." You may be thinking this, but you will never be able to avoid it forever.

You may never be on a stage talking to thousands, but you do have to speak to the public in many different ways.

Public speaking can also be called presentation skills or persuasive speaking. It is a skill set that most people do not have and aren't willing to learn. So by committing to master this skill; it sets you apart from everyone else. If public speaking truly is the #1 fear of most people and you are willing to work past it, then there isn't much else to fear after you tackle this one.

What is Public Speaking?

My definition of public speaking is when you address a group of people no matter how small. It can be asked to present information to your boss, your team, or a larger group of people. Public speaking is when you are put on the spot with all eyes in the room listening to what you say and watching how you present yourself!

It is more than just standing in front of a group of people, public speaking is also how you can influence others or persuade them to understand or support your point of view.

> *Public speaking is how you can persuade others to understand or support your point of view.*

There are many different ways public speaking skills are helpful to your career and your personal life. Here are a few examples:

You are asked in front of a team meeting to communicate status updates about a project

- The executive team asks you to give a report of your team's performance
- As a business owner you want to market your business using videos
- Your best friend asks you to deliver an entertaining toast at a wedding
- You teach a workshop for other experts in your industry
- It is your annual performance review and you want to ask for a raise

Speaking to your boss about a raise with eloquence and using the correct body language is public speaking. Speaking in front of as few as three people in a meeting room is considered public speaking. Now think about your typical day...how many times do you have to captivate an audience with what you say? Heck, having a family meeting and trying to persuade my kids to follow the weekly chore list is public speaking. The techniques used in this book will help you succeed in any speaking situation.

Why Should You Master the Skill of Speaking in Public?

I used to think that I could avoid public speaking. In fact, I was a writer and training program developer in a restaurant training department in 2003. I was developing an 8-week manager training program for the front of the house managers and kitchen managers. The company was having a big meeting in Las Vegas with all the Vice Presidents and Director of Operations. My boss was going to present my new training program for their feedback and approval. I spent two days prepping my boss on the training program and how to present the material. We reviewed the reasons why we needed a change in our manager programs, the differences of the two programs, the layout of the materials, and how it will increase manager performance and lower manager turnover, etc. Two days before the meeting, my boss calls me and says, "Cheryl, after days of cramming this information, I don't think I can convey the message as well as you. After all, this is your creation and as the creator you know all the details that I will never know. I booked you a flight to Vegas and you will have one and a half hours to present the new training program." I had never taken a course on public speaking or addressed a group larger than 5 – 8 people in a meeting, and I had never presented to executives before.

My heart began to pound as the panic set in, and my mind began racing. What? I am leaving in two days? I have no time to practice? The room is filled with big wigs!

I must fill one and a half hours? I can't breathe! I think I am going to pass out!

Anxiety and panic set in and I will never forget that feeling. To calm down I tried to stop the crazy thoughts and negative self-talk by focusing on my breathing to get through the shock. Breathe in slowly and then count to ten on the exhale. Talk about being put on the spot! Well, I did the best I could and honestly it went really well. But from that moment on…I wanted to master the art of public speaking with no panic attacks! It is a good thing I did, because my career moved in the direction of presenting at annual company conferences and teaching workshops for National Associations immediately after that meeting.

So if you think you can avoid public speaking and you will never have to address a large group…never say never! You can't predict the future and I don't want you to go through the panic I felt.

Even though your health and stress level alone is a good reason to master this skill, I have 8 reasons why you need to master the art of presentation skills.

Reason #1: At some point in your life, you will need to do it, just like I did!

Almost every single person will be required to speak in public at some point in their career. Every public speaking opportunity is an opportunity to grow your leadership reputation, learn how to influence others, and define yourself as an expert in your company or industry.

By becoming a confident and comfortable public speaker you instantly put yourself above the others who refuse to stand up to speak and do it well. Let's face it...the ones that learn this skill and stand in front of the room are the ones considered the most successful in business. Don't you want to be a leader in your industry and stand out from the crowd?

So don't be naïve like I used to be and think you will never have to deliver a speech. You might be in network marketing and need to conduct a presentation about your business, you may need to do a sales presentation about a product, or you might have to give a speech at your daughter's wedding. No matter who you are it is almost 100% certain you will need to give a speech at some point in your life. Don't you want to be ready?

Reason #2: Public speaking separates the men from the boys and the divas from the girls.

As we have established the majority of people will avoid public speaking in any given situation. By having the confidence and ability to speak in public you can differentiate yourself in your industry. This could put you in line for the next promotion; it could get you more sign ups in your network marketing business, or keep your head off the chopping block when your company has their next round of lay-offs.

Reason #3: Mastering public speaking is one of the best ways to generate sales (or get a better job).

Understanding how to effectively get your message (and the emotions tied to that message) across to another person can help you generate more sales for your company or business.

When you are comfortable speaking in front of groups and you do it well, you become a leader in your industry. Business owners need to meet with other experts in their industry with the Chamber of Commerce or other networking groups.

Reason #4: Presentation skills increase your self-confidence in all areas of life.

Public speaking has a tendency to transform you from a normal person to feeling like a super hero. It can dramatically increase your self-confidence and self-esteem. It is unfortunate, but a lot of our self-worth is gained by the perception others have about our skills, knowledge, and competence.

When you master public speaking, you are able to communicate your message with more clarity. So in general conversation you can better understand what people are thinking and then change what you are saying to make them think and feel the way you want them to. You will learn the skill of persuasion and work it to your advantage.

Reason #5: Learning persuasive speaking is a great way to get a promotion or a better job.

Public speaking skills are important in securing a better job or getting a promotion. It is how you present yourself at a job interview that will be the ultimate decider as to whether or not you land that higher paying job and whether or not you get paid from the lower bracket of pay rates.

You can get that promotion you have been wanting because public speaking shows off your ability to lead a large team! You can gain the confidence to ask your boss for a raise because you can eloquently share your performance results and the reasons you deserve the raise.

Reason #6: Public speaking will help you form a community of supporters.

By standing in front of an audience and presenting information, you can attract like-minded people. Leaders have people rally around them. As your community grows so can your sales. Once you have a loyal fan base following you, then you can continue to reach them immediately through your Facebook fan page, email communication, offering a free webinar, and more.

Reason #7: Public speaking allows you to demonstrate your knowledge and improve upon your knowledge.

By having the courage to stand up and speak to a crowd you are positioning yourself as an expert in your field, and it gives you a great opportunity to share your knowledge.

To stay an expert in your field, you need to learn is to teach. Public speaking is exactly that…an opportunity to teach. Public speaking is important because it helps you to improve your knowledge. The preparation that goes into a speech and the fact you have to practice how to communicate key points effectively to others makes you understand your content that much better.

Reason #8: Presentation skills can boost performance in other areas of your life.

Public speaking will improve your communication skills, your leadership skills, your confidence, and your ability to read and understand people. You will gain a skill of being able to comprehend others body language. You will be able to know what they are thinking and what they are about to say just by watching their reactions. These skills are transferrable when raising your kids and communicating difficult situations with your spouse.

EXERCISE: Why is it important for YOU to master public speaking? Think about your goals and how public speaking can help you stand out from others.

1. What goals can I achieve faster if I have the skill of public speaking?

2. Which one of these reasons best describes my reason for learning public speaking?

3. What is holding me back from mastering the skill of presenting information to a group?

4. Where will I be in five years in my business/career if I don't master this skill?

How to Manage Stage Fright

No one is a stranger to fear. Fear can start at a young age. From fear of the dark and needing to sleep with a nightlight, to worrying there is a monster under the bed. As we grow up, other fears seem to sprout.

What do you fear the most in life? I am fearful of creepy, hairy spiders, horror movies, and slithering snakes. When I think about these things my skin crawls. Many women are fearful of never getting married while the men seem to be afraid of commitment. LOL! I went on the search for the top 10 biggest fears and I expected our expiration date or death to be the biggest fear but it wasn't.

I was completely shocked when I learned that public speaking was in the top 5 of most fear lists. Public speaking was a greater fear than death. What? When I found this out, I had been conducting training meetings from the small size of 30 to being on a larger stage speaking to 1200 people. I remember when I first had to get in front of a group and speak. I was so nervous; my palms were sweating, my hands visually shaking, and my stomach in knots.

Jerry Seinfeld made a great joke based on a simple observation:

"I read a thing that actually says that speaking in front of a crowd is considered the number one fear of the average person. I found that amazing – number two was death! **That means to the average person if you have to be at a funeral, you would rather be in the casket than doing the eulogy."**

I think people are afraid to speak in front of others for many valid reasons, but I haven't found a book or training that made this learning process easy. Public speaking is a talent that can be learned, no one is born with this skill. No matter who you are, you will have to do it sometime so why not be ready.

So why do you fear public speaking? Take this seriously and put some thought into your answer. Then write down all the things you fear will or can happen while you are speaking to a group.

_____

_____

_____

_____

_____

_____

Congratulations! Defining your fear is the first step to facing it. When you face it, then you can send fear running in the opposite direction.

So why do the majority of people fear public speaking? I posted this question on Facebook and here were some of the most popular answers I received. Do your answers match any of these fears?

"Fear of looking like a fool or saying the wrong thing." -Tony

"I am uncomfortable if I'm unfamiliar with the topic or not passionate about the subject." -Jennifer

"I hate public speaking...it makes me sick. For me it's because I feel people are judging me." -Jen

"Fear of saying something that would embarrass me in front of hundreds or thousands." -Cory

"I am afraid my mind will go blank and I won't remember any of my presentation." -Renee

These are the standard fears, so if you can relate, then you aren't alone. I too had all the above feelings and now I love speaking in front of others.

So how do you get over these fears? Just like anything else, you need to learn presentation skills just like you learned your multiplication tables in elementary. You can learn these skills just as easily as you learned math. Once you learn the skills, you have to put them into practice to get rid of the fear. You have to put yourself out there, over and over again!

Forcing yourself out of your comfort zone is the only way you will ever grow new skills. The best way to get over your fear of public speaking is to continue to try it. Okay, you don't like that answer. I didn't either, but it is true!

Fear of public speaking can be paralyzing to people and can even cause someone to become physically ill. This paralyzing fear is created by the misconception of what you should look like, sound like, and act like. Many of these thoughts are flat out lies, so let's shed some truth on the subject shall we?

I want to address the top paralyzing fears that stop someone in their tracks of public speaking. I want you to see that when you change your perception about the fear, then the fear itself can disappear. When you take these fear busters into consideration, you will begin to gain confidence.

Paralyzing Fear #1: Fear of rejection and being made fun of!

Fear Buster #1: You will not be liked by everyone and not everyone will relate to your speaking style.

I was watching Joel Osteen one Saturday and he was talking about getting people to like you. There are people pleasers out there that want everyone to like them. One of my best friends is a people pleaser and she would get so stressed out when she felt like she did something wrong.

This created a lot of additional stress in her life. I had a tendency to want other's approval also. I believe that most of us at some point in our life have desired the approval from others.

Joel Osteen said and I paraphrase… "Did you know that no matter what you do, even if you didn't do anything wrong, 25% of the people you come into contact with won't like you?"

That statement made me stop and think. No matter what I do? Even if I was perfect and said all the right things…25% STILL wouldn't like me? Since I wanted to let go of the stress of trying to please everyone, I quickly adopted this philosophy as my own.

I came to the conclusion, "Why would I waste time thinking about the people that wouldn't support me or make fun of me?" I should focus on the people that will listen and ask for more. Those are the people that are most important to me anyway.

I would say over and over in my mind to change my perception, *"Not everyone is going to like what I have to say, but my goal isn't to please everyone. It is to help the ones that will listen and can relate."* Now you repeat it and start believing it!

Paralyzing Fear #2: Fearing the audience's expectation of what they will learn.

Fear Buster #2: Your audience may know a lot about the topic you are teaching but they haven't heard your valuable viewpoint and haven't seen it delivered with your personality style.

The fear of the audience expectation is living up to the audience's expectation of the value of your message. The other part of this fear is not looking like a credible source or that maybe your audience knows more about your topic than you do. This is just crazy thinking! Everyone has different viewpoints, and a different way of sharing their message. If you Google the subject 'public speaking', you may find similarities in the content, but I guarantee you will gain different insight from each article.

Every person has a different personality which creates a unique viewpoint and a diverse way of delivering a message. Don't worry about the audience's expectation; you need to be happy with your message. When you are passionate about your material, you will radiate confidence and the audience will perceive you as a credible source.

So I trained my brain to believe, *"My audience may know a lot about the subject, but they don't have my professional insight and unique know-how. They will learn one or two new things and that is all the value they need."*

You may be thinking, they only need to learn two or three new things? Is that even worth it? Yes, it is. In a blog article by Jack Malcolm, "How Much of Your Presentation Will They Remember?" he shared some research.

Researchers once ran a test to measure how much of a presenter's message sticks in the minds of their audience. They found that immediately after a 10-minute presentation, listeners only remembered 50% of what was said. By the next day that had dropped to 25%, and a week later it was 10%.

Most people cannot learn more than one or two things and implement those into their daily routine. Anything above and beyond three messages becomes clutter.

Paralyzing Fear #3: Fear of being judged.

Fear Buster #3: Judgment is human nature and can't be avoided.

You are judged on a daily basis, and yes, you judge others every day. You don't hibernate in your home and avoid going out in public because of this do you? Then why would you avoid mastering something that could put you ahead of all these judgmental people?

There was a study that shown people will make 11 judgments about you within the first seven seconds of meeting you. Don't let that scare you...because if they are doing it to you, then you are doing it to them. Ha!

Like I said before, judging is human nature, whether it is right or wrong. Here is the positive side of it. When people are judging you; they are they paying attention to you. If they are paying attention to you, they are deciding how they feel about you. The type of person I judged quickly is a comedian.

I will use Jeff Foxworthy for my example. I grew up in Oklahoma, and my goal growing up was to NEVER have a redneck accent. So when I first heard Jeff Foxworthy's jokes, "You might be a redneck if…" I thought to myself, he sounds like he rode the short bus to school with that accent. Based on my goals and my perception of having an Oklahoma accent, my judgment was he wasn't funny or smart. That couldn't be further from the truth.

Based on my first impression of Jeff Foxworthy, I placed negative judgments about his accent and his choice of material. Now even though I didn't appreciate his redneck jokes, millions of people did. After a period of time, he started to rub off on me, and now I can appreciate the differences between the two of us and find humor in his jokes.

So is this putting you as ease or just creating more fear about judgment? I believe the majority of the time, you can win people over when given the chance.

There was a girl at one of my jobs that really disliked me, and I felt the same as her. Neither of us kept it a secret! We would glare at each other when passing in the halls. We worked in the same department and we were paired up to travel the United States to teach an 'exciting' class of 'sexual harassment in the workplace'. I will never forget when this announcement was made. We were sitting right next to each other and we slowly moved our heads to make eye contact with each other.

At the same time we both rolled our eyes at each other following with a long sigh. We were going on the road together; flying on the same plane, riding for hours in the same rental car, and staying at the same hotels. It was going to be torture! On our first trip, we discovered we were sorority sisters, we had the same sarcastic sense of humor, and our favorite drink was a dirty martini. We went from enemies to BFF's. We still laugh to this day how silly it was that we both thought, "She thinks she is better than me." Now my husband and I go on vacation with her and her husband every year.

You can't worry if people are judging you or making fun of you. Either way, you made an impression large enough that they are spending time thinking and talking about YOU! Time is precious to everyone; we never have enough of it. So focus on the ones that like you not the ones that don't.

Paralyzing Fear #4: The fear of making mistakes.

Fear Buster #4: You will make mistakes and that is just fine, no one expects perfection. The mistake isn't as important as your response to the mistake.

The best way to deal with mistakes is to embrace the moment by having fun when you make it. Nobody expects perfection and that is good, because your presentation will never be perfect.

I was raised in a home of two perfectionists! Let me give you a few examples…

I received an email through Facebook from my Dad the other day that corrected a typo I had on my Facebook wall. Yes, I know the difference between "by" and "buy"; I have a college degree and make six figures! My Dad couldn't let that mistake go without letting me know he knew I made a mistake. Come on, we all have typos using an iPhone.

My Mom organizes her DVD movies by actor and actress. She even makes little labels that stick out from the DVD's with the actor's name so the movies are categorized clearly. She also has a typed up list of movies by actor and another list by movie title. Do you think there is a little OCD in my family?

Trying to be perfect has been an expectation and a curse, but now that I am getting older, I know perfection isn't possible. So now, when I make mistakes I accept them and move on. When they happen in front of other people, I just laugh with them. I think the more mistakes I make the more the audience likes me. They see that I have a sense of humor and they can relate to some of their embarrassing moments. I become more real to them and they feel a connection. A connection can build trust, which helps the group to perceive you as competent and credible.

Paralyzing Fear #5: Fear of forgetting your material.

Fear Buster #5: You may forget the perfect way to say something, but you will NOT forget your presentation.

I am a big believer in practicing your presentation. I go it a little overboard sometimes when I practice, but I want to ensure that I am 100% ready to deliver a great presentation. I don't believe in wasting other's time. Because people are so worried about making a mistake or saying something wrong, they try to memorize the material. Memorizing the material can actually backfire on you. When you memorize content, you place an expectation on yourself that you need to say it just the way the speech written. In reality, you should know your material very well and be able to flow through it without looking at any support material, yet you don't have to say it just like it is written on paper.

Here is a secret…the audience don't know if you aren't following your speech. They don't know if you make a mistake or say something wrong unless you tell them. Now I am not talking about misquoting or representing facts & figures, I am talking about saying something the exact way that you wrote it or practiced it.

When you place too much pressure on yourself to say something perfecting then maybe my self-talk with help you. My perception self-talk is… *"I wrote this content, and even though I may not say it the exact way I wrote or practiced it…the audience will never know. To them, that was just the way I planned it. The most important thing is I am able to clearly communicate my points to the audience."*

After years and years of presenting, I still get butterflies. I can still get nervous! Yet it is a controlled nervous, because it is energy.

Without these feelings, my passion can't come out and neither can my energy. You want to be in a place where you control your fears and they don't control you! Sometimes, that fear is what will push you do to better!

EXERCISE: To become comfortable with public speaking, it starts with how you prepare your mind and learning to embrace your personal style. You need to start preparing your mind and changing the perception of your fear.

For these five fears we just discussed, I have included a self-talk phrase which is a positive affirmation that I would repeat over and over to myself until I believed it. Review the fears you wrote down previously and write down your positive self-talk phrase that you will repeat to change your viewpoint and drive away your fear.

Fear: _____

Positive Self-talk:

_____

_____

Fear: _____

Positive Self-talk:

_____

_____

Fear: _____

Positive Self-talk:

_____

_____

Learning to Calm the Nerves

If you get nervous when speaking in front of other people, then you are normal. Even the expert speaker's blood pressure increases and their heart pumps a little faster. The difference is how you respond to your body's reaction.

When you begin to feel the anxiety or excitement, will you convert that into productive energy or will you clam up and allow yourself to fear? The key to learning how to cope with your feelings and calm your nerves is to turn the anxiety feeling into healthy excitement. If you doubt this can be accomplished then don't, it can be done with some practice and the correct mindset adjustment.

Part of turning anxiety into healthy energy is to learn what will relax you. The main goal is to prevent anxiety from occurring at all. The most common answer on how to calm your nerves before a presentation is to picture your audience naked. Now I don't know who came up with that solution but that would spin me into a panic attack that I wouldn't recover from. So I recommend that you don't focus on the audience but you focus on yourself.

There are 5 tactics that may help you to control your nerves and anxiety.

1. Practice, practice, practice

> 66 Practice does not make perfect. Only perfect practice makes perfect. – *Vince Lombardi*

When you spend time preparing yourself it gives you a boost of confidence because you know the material. When you get put on the spot and have nothing prepared is when your anxiety can be at an all-time high. So if you know you have a meeting presentation or a speech to give then take the time to practice.

One trick that I use is I always practice in front of a mirror. It feels really weird at first and it may cause you to forget what you are talking about but it works wonders. Why does it work? Because practicing in a room with no one looking at you isn't realistic. When you practice in front of a mirror you are seeing a face look back at you and that can be the most awkward part of getting comfortable speaking in front of a group. It is those sets of eyes staring at you that can create panic.

Recording yourself on video is incredibly helpful. It is so simple now that we have smart phones. Just prop your phone on a tripod and then begin to share your message.

After you finished recording watch yourself on video, and immediately begin making improvements to your delivery skills. Other than practicing in front of friends, video can be your best tool.

2. Personal Calming Tricks

Everyone is different and has to find their trick to calm their surging energy. For some people it involves counting slowly to 10 while they breathe in and out. Maybe making a fist over and over again will work out the nerves. Pacing back and forth works for many although that just makes me more nervous.

I slap on the headphones and jam out to a motivating song. I listen to the lyrics that make me feel unstoppable, maybe the theme from "Rocky". I also take a quiet time for prayer 10 minutes before I approach a group.

You know yourself very well, so find the couple of things that really help you prepare yourself and that calm your anxiety and nerves.

EXERCISE: What are some ideas that you want to try to calm your nerves. Write them down below and give each of them a try, and then you can stick to the ones that do the trick.

_____

_____

_____

_____

_____

_____

3. Start Strong

Having a solid start or opening can instantly link you to your audience and get the presentation off to a great start. Remember, you typically only have 20 to 30 seconds to capture the group's attention so make it good.

When you have a winning opening statement, this can instantly calm your nerves in the first few minutes no matter how you felt when you started.

Here are a few opening ideas that can set the stage for success while allowing your personality to shine through at the same time.

- What's In It for Them (WIIFM). Most people only care themselves and what they will gain from the presentation. So tell them how your information will benefit their business or life.

- Personal Story or Scenario. People love to get to know more about speakers, so you can share a story or real-life scenario that relates to your training topic.

- Numbers Don't Lie. Sharing an unusual statistic that relates to the audience or training topic.

- Powerful Quote. Most people love quotes. This is a no-brainer if you spend any time on Facebook, Twitter, Instagram, or Pinterest.

- Video Clip. When showing a video clip make sure it isn't longer than 2 minutes. In the video the point needs to be early in the video to capture their attention in the first 30 seconds.

4. Build in Answers for Anticipated Questions

One of the best ways to keep the audience engaged is to encourage them to ask questions. Some people are nervous about answering questions so the best idea is to write down all the questions you think your audience will be thinking about and then include those answers in your speech.

One of the ways to be able to get information is to ask in advance when possible. If you can't email audience members then speak with the person in charge of the meeting or event and get information from them that way. Two of the questions that are most important to learn is what keeps them up at night or what is their biggest challenge? You want to provide solutions and to do that you must know their problems.

5. Positive Self-Talk

If you continue to tell yourself that you are scared and aren't ready to speak in front of a crowd then that is exactly what you will get. You will never overcome your anxiety and move past the point of mastering public speaking. You must say positive comments about yourself and to yourself. You need to prepare statements that you say over and over again, and yes the more you repeat it the sooner you will believe it.

"I am prepared and I know more about the subject than the attendees I am teaching."

"A little nervous energy is good; it will help be bring enthusiasm to my speech."

"The group will be attentive and interested in what I am saying."

"This will be a fun experience."

We all have an established thinking pattern that can either work against us or encourage us. Make sure you don't make learning the skill of public speaking harder than it needs to be. You need to be a fan in your own corner to control your nerves.

EXERCISE:

1. Close your eyes and relax for a minute. I want you to think about the last time you spoke in front of a group or people. What were some of the things you said to yourself or thought about yourself? Write those self-talk statements below.

2. Now let's change that attitude and create a positive self-talk statement to replace your anxiety thoughts.

3. Write those positive self-talk statements on a notecard and carry them with you to your next speech. You can also review them every time you practice your speech.

Chapter 2

Discover Your Personal Style

*You can speak well if your tongue can
deliver the message of your heart.*
~John Ford

Stop Being a Speaker & Be Yourself

For the past 20+ years, I spent it working and
networking in the training industry. What I love about the
industry is that trainers truly appreciate each other just the
way they are. Trainers are corky, crazy, high-energy, and fun
to be around. Most importantly, they all have their own style
of training, teaching and presenting. To be successful in
public speaking you shouldn't try to speak like anybody else,
but you do need to embrace your personal style.

If you research other speakers to watch different
presenter's delivery, and then be careful not to begin to act
and talk like them.

You will like some of their styles so much that you want to be like them. So you will try to mimic their style. I remember watching a friend of mine on stage and he was so energetic and funny. The crowd loved him and so did I. I wanted to present just like him and have the same ability to make an audience laugh. His presentation sounded like he didn't have speaker notes. He sounded like he was having a private conversation with me even though there were more than 300 other trainers in the room. The next time I taught a class I tried to match his energy level and humor style and I flopped. Why? Because I wasn't being myself, I was trying to mimic someone else.

So you need to develop your OWN style! People will appreciate you being real! Besides, when you try to act like someone else it looks awkward to the crowd because it is uncomfortable for you. So to be comfortable and successful with your own style, then you need to learn about your strengths and how your qualities will capture the audience's attention.

If you aren't confident that you know what your best qualities are and how they can shine while speaking in public, then let's go through some exercises that can help you.

What are your natural qualities? You can start by making a list of your strengths, for instance – funny, integrity, honest, intense, and knowledgeable. You can use those qualities while you are presenting. There is a tendency for speakers to think they have to act a certain way. Resist the temptation to try and act like a professional speaker and just be person your close friends know and love. List your strengths below:

_____   _____

_____   _____

_____   _____

_____   _____

_____   _____

_____   _____

_____   _____

You gotta be you. Everyone has unique and quirky behaviors. Allow the quirky aspects of your personality to be a part of your speaking or performing style. Those personality quirks will be the marks of authenticity that your audience perceives with the eyes and ears of their hearts.

Let your style be based on your natural rhythms. Introverts and extraverts have different rhythms for expression. Introverts are deep and inwardly focused, so their thoughts and words come from the depths of their thoughts and feelings. If you are an introvert, let yourself speak slowly, deliberately, and thoughtfully. Don't try to manufacture enthusiasm that is false for you. Extraverts are dynamic and outwardly focused. If you are extraverted, be large and dramatic. Don't try to squash your natural energies or be too controlled.

Say it like you would say it in real life. Speak, present or perform just like you are talking to friends in your living room. Ask yourself, "How would I really say this?" Then say it that way, just as if you were talking to a close friend. The audience wants to relate with you not the idea of someone you are trying to be like.

Give up trying to be perfect. Let your style be imperfect. Don't try to complete your speaker notes with no mistakes. That isn't realistic and isn't natural. Instead of trying to speak perfectly, focus on speaking the truth. When you tell the truth, you don't speak in literary phrases. You let it come from your heart as you feel it.

Realize that being perfect does not equate to being effective. Being effective does not have to do with your performance. It has to do with what happens to the listeners as a result of who you are being with them.

Make space for your fear. Give yourself permission to feel your fear, anxiety or tension when you are presenting and performing. The fear is energy; it is power and passion. When you create space inside yourself to feel the fear, it converts into passion that causes your words to vibrate with electricity.

Delivery Styles

There are different ways to prepare you to deliver a memorable speech. So you want to choose the best strategy based on your personality. I am a little OCD so details matter to me Spending a lot of time writing out speaker notes, practicing in front of the mirror is a must for me to feel confident and comfortable prior to standing on stage. Some people are better at delivering based on an idea and not having all their speaker notes written in detail.

There isn't a right way or wrong way to prepare yourself with the exception of choosing the best strategy that suits your personality. Here are a few delivery styles that you can choose from.

Impromptu Delivery (Ad-libbed)

When speakers use this style they do not spend a lot of time preparing the exact wording of their speech. They spend more of their time preparing the ideas they want to present, and then decides the exact way to present them. Presenters that use this delivery style may often prepare notes in an outline form that contains the main ideas of their training and additional bullet notes for each main point.

Script Delivery

In the script delivery style the speaker writes an entire speech in advance. This can be useful when you must ensure the presentation doesn't run over a certain amount of time. In this style, the speaker is referring to their notes more often and in some ways reading from their document or script. This delivery style has many drawbacks and is the least engaging for the audience to watch. This style prevents the speaker from making eye contact with the audience, and has difficultly reading and reacting to the audience's reactions.

Memorized Delivery

When a memorized delivery style is used, the speaker writes out a complete speech manuscript and then commits it to memory word for word. This allows speakers to make eye contact with the audience and concentrate on their nonverbal gestures. However, this speaking style has its challenges, such as the long amount of time it can take to memorize a speech and the possibility that it will be forgotten during the presentation.

For me I combine a few of these delivery methods. I start with an outline so I have a great overview of my entire presentation. Then I write out my speech in sentence form and begin reading it over and over. When I practice I speak from the heart ensuring I get my key points across to the audience and I don't worry about saying it just as I have it written down.

No matter which style you choose the most important factor is that you deliver value to your audience, entertainment to keep them engaged, and respond to their reactions. You will need to plan, prepare, and practice for any of these delivery methods just some methods require more preparation than others.

Forms of Communication

If you had three words in your mind on how the audience would describe your presentation skills, what would they be? What descriptive words would you want them to say about you after watching your speech?

Write these descriptor words down.

_____

_____

_____

As you prepare yourself and practice, keep these words fresh in your mind. These words describe the lasting impression you want to leave with the audience, and they describe your goals as a presenter.

When preparing a presentation there are more important factors than WHAT you say. I know this may be hard to believe but your body language and tone of voice is more important than the words you speak.

In fact, there was a study done that determined body language and tone of voice is more important to capture the audience' attention than the actual words spoken.

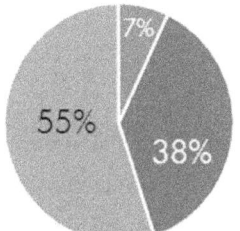

Elements of Personal Communication
- 7% spoken words
- 38% voice, tone
- 55% body language

There are many nonverbal forms of communication that give a clear meaning without using any words; for example, blowing a kiss, winking, rolling the eyes, etc.

Think about the impact of non-verbal communication for a minute. We have a tendency to focus on a person's behavior as the truth more than someone's words. If you are a parent I am sure you have told your child 'no' before. They probably had a sad or even mad look on their face, but when you ask them if they are 'okay'; they respond with their arms crossed, pouty mouth, and say "I am finnnnnneeeee"! Now your kid's words say that everything is okay yet their tone of voice and body language screams they are unhappy with your decision.

As a speaker your audience will interpret what you say based on your body language and tone of voice more than the words you say.

Proper Body Language

There are many tricks to delivery your presentation with the proper body language. Let's go through each of them and give you some pointers.

<u>Hand Gestures</u>

Your hand gestures add a lot of emphasis and emotion to your speaking, just as your voice does. Knowing how to control your hands in a positive manner can be one of the best things you pay attention to for polished delivery. Gestures can be substitutes for words in some situations, but mostly are used for added emphasis. Here are some tips and tricks to help you from distracting the audience from what you are teaching.

Distracting Hand Gestures: These are movements that may annoy the audience or cause them to pay attention to your movements more than what you say. Avoid speaking with your hands in your pocket, playing with hair; arms crossed or behind your back, or leaning on the podium.

Effective Hand Gestures: When presenting in front of a group, use hand gestures to highlight key points. Remember to keep the gestures large as the audience can't see small movements, especially in a big room. Be animated, but in control. You can watch yourself in the mirror while you practice presenting and you can see what your arms are doing which can help you see from the audience point of view.

Facial Gestures and Eye Contact

Facial gestures also need review and particular attention. Your face and eyes show the emotion that you are truly feeling, often without knowing you are expressing them. Practicing facial emotions in front of a mirror or a video recorder can help you see what emotions are really coming across. In general, try the following tips to help improve your facial gestures and eye contact:

Eye Contact: What were the looks on the faces of the audience? Well you won't know if you don't maintain eye contact with every section of the room! Your goal is for every person in the room to feel that you have looked them personally in the eye. You can do this by maintaining constant eye contact with your audience. Look an audience member for a couple of seconds, and then turn to someone else. Some speakers have recommended that you look right above the audience's eyes on their forehead or just above their heads. You do not want to do this. The audience can tell when you aren't looking them in the eyes. You could risk losing their attention by not showing confidence by giving them direct eye contact.

Genuine Smile: Try to have a natural smile while you are talking. This shows the audience that you are happy to be there and you like them. When you force a smile, the audience can tell. It will cause your audience to feel uncomfortable with you as a speaker.

Facial Expressions: Show energy and enthusiasm through your facial expressions. Most speakers no matter how experienced will get a natural adrenaline rush before entering the stage. Channel this energy outward so the audience can see you are excited to be there. The speakers that can do this may even see the audience sit taller in their seats and move towards the front of their chair. It will look like they are hanging on your every word. If you portray low energy it will cause the audience to become bored and they will tune you out.

Body Positioning

The way you position your body in front of the audience will convey nonverbal messages. For example, if you are to stand in front of your audience with your hands folded over in front of your body, it may look like you are closed off or unhappy to be there.

Standing in the Correct Location: Get out from behind podium. Great presenters work the crowd and/or stage. However, try not to turn your back on the audience when using a screen with PowerPoint. If you are in the crowd and heading back to the front of the room or stage, walk backwards slowly and be careful. Your goal is to face the audience as much as possible avoiding them seeing your back.

Proper Body Posture: Stand tall and have proper body posture. Great posture is a sign of confidence. Don't slouch or lean on a podium or table.

Body Movement

Certain movement during a presentation can be distracting, especially if you have a nervous "tick" or adapter. Rocking back and forth during a presentation is a common nervous adapter and occurs because the adrenaline rushing through your body needs an outlet for energy. Creating a movement pattern can help channel this energy and help keep focus and control of the random movement that could be a distraction. Be aware of nervous adapters through movement like shaky legs, nervous side-step, weight shifting, standing with your feet crossed, rocking forward and back, and any other nervous unnecessary movement. Practice your movement until it looks natural, and you know you will have the nervous movement adapters under control.

Vocal Quality

Body language and vocal quality are the two components responsible for over 80% of the audience members' perception of your effectiveness. So you need to make sure that your vocal quality compliments your body language and the stories you are sharing.

Voice Pitch: Vary your pitch and tone to keep the audience engaged; avoid monotone or robotic speech; speak loudly or use a microphone. The pitch of your voice can show your audience that you are excited about being there and passionate about your subject. If you are passionate about what you are teaching then they will be excited to listen.

Voice Volume: The loudness of your voice matters too. If you are in a small business meeting with only 10 people, then you won't speak as loud as if you are standing in a larger room with 30 people. If you have 40+ people in a room then use a microphone so you can speak at a normal volume yet the entire room can hear you clearly. It is difficult to listen to a person that has to raise their voice to be heard in a big room.

Pace of your Speech: Most people talk at over 100 words per minute without being nervous – practice, practice, practice to ensure you do not go too fast during the session. The group will feel rushed and may miss important points. If you naturally speak fast, then you will feel like you are talking in slow motion which for the audience will seem like a normal speed. Don't allow your nerves to speed up your speech where your audience doesn't retain your information. Remember, if you are training on a subject your audience will probably be taking notes so pay attention to your audience's reactions. If they are looking around at other people's notes, then you need to slow down. Also, speaking too slowly can also become a problem for your audience. If your words drag on for them, it gives the audience too much time to process other thoughts while you are speaking. Practice in front of a small group of friends and find out if you have a tendency to speak too fast or too slow and practice making those adjustments.

Dramatic Pause: Pauses refer to a stop in speaking. They can add dramatic emphasis and prepare the audience for following material that is of some importance. Pauses create places for your audience to stop and take a breather when information gets heavy with content or emotion. They also create places for them to refocus on your information and go deeper into the content or emotion that you are presenting. Be careful not to over-do the length of pauses you are using as they can cause awkwardness with your audience as well, leaving them to wonder when you will start to speak again. If your pause is too quick, your audience won't catch that you wanted them to have a moment for digestion and the additional emphasis won't be gained. Decide where you want these pauses for added emphasis and pencil them in on your speaking notes.

Avoid Filler Words: Make your words relevant! Avoid those filler words such as um, uh, you know, whatever, okay, and so on. You are only saying those words because you think you can't have silence or pauses while you are speaking. Taking your time to breathe or have silence is fine and encouraged. When you practice and memorize what you are going to say it will help eliminate many of these words. Know the presentation so you can deliver it versus deciding what you will say next and adding unnecessary words.

Appearance and Dress

The way you dress will affect your first impression with the audience. If you are dressed professionally, your audience will expect a professional message. If you are dressed sloppily, your audience will have lower expectation. The way you dress can affect your credibility with the audience.

Part of having confidence during the presentation is also due to dressing for success. Give attention to all details of this outfit, down to your jewelry, socks, and shoes. Likewise, make sure your physical appearance looks and smells clean, professional, and polished.

Find out the attire, dress code, or culture of your audience, and ensure you are properly dressed for the presentation. For example, if you were asked to speak at a corporate Harley Davidson conference, showing up in a suit may cause you to look like a nerd. Of course, presenting to a corporate conference for another company in Harley Davidson gear would cause you to look unprofessional.

Delivery Checklist

Place a check by each item after you have reviewed it in preparation of your speech delivery.

_____I have created a full content manuscript outline and have done a number of timed rehearsals with it.

_____I have created speaking notes and revised them so that they have information I know I will need during my actual presentation.

_____I have timed my speech repeatedly using speaking notes until I am confident I will not go over or under the speaking time limits.

_____I have practiced using my visual aids with my speech a number of times.

_____I have identified places for a movement pattern in my speech and have practiced in a similar room so that I know how spread apart my stops will be.

_____I have identified specific places in my speech to incorporate facial, body, and hand gestures for more impact.

_____I have practiced eye contact by giving my speech to other people, videotaping myself, and/or giving my speech in front of a mirror.

_____I feel confident I can look people in the eye during quotes, sources, introduction, and conclusion especially.

_____I have practiced facial expressions in the mirror for further emotional impact and feel confident I can smile comfortably and look relaxed.

_____I have a professional business style outfit picked out to wear for my public speech.

_____I have identified my potential nervous adapters and have made precautions to reduce tendencies to display them.

Chapter 3

Captivating the Audience

There are three things to aim at in public speaking: first, get into your subject, and then get your subject into yourself, and lastly, to get your subject into the heart of your audience.
~Alexander Gregg

Knowing Your Audience

Understanding what the audience needs and how they learn will help you when developing your presentation. In fact, this is probably one of the most important areas because without the audience there is no need for you to create a presentation right? And more importantly, if your audience doesn't believe your material is relevant to their situation then they don't learn anything.

An effective public speaker understands their audience and adapts their presentation accordingly. In order to do this, you must learn everything you can about your particular audience. Then make sure to keep the audience in mind in every decision you make during the creation and writing process. When focusing on understanding the audience, you find common traits that enable you to identify with them and their needs. Since audiences are concerned with things that they believe will directly affect them, it's your job to find as many different ways that your topic relates to your particular audience. The more ways you can find to connect with the audience, the more reasons they have to listen to you. Whenever possible you want to learn about the audience demographics, the environment of the training area, the outlook on the topic you are teaching, and any background or culture of the company.

Demographics

While understanding that demographic information can be very helpful, be careful to fall into a danger zone of stereotyping. Demographics information should be used as a tool and you should not completely reply on the information.

Age: An audience in their 20's will have different interests, views on a subject, and motivations than one in their 70's. Their viewpoints will be different based on what was happening in the world while they were growing up.

Education Level: Is your audience filled with people holding advanced degrees, or are they mainly high school graduates? Maybe your audience is mixed?

Occupation: What does your audience do for a living? Do they all share similar jobs or work for the same company? Can you somehow connect your topic to their jobs?

Gender: The gender of the audience will matter when putting together your stories. For example, a presentation that uses only sports analogies would be less effective for an all-female audience.

Marital status: Is your audience mainly married, single, or divorced? These groups will have different values and motivations. How about children? Parents have different challenges and hobbies than someone that has never been married and doesn't have children.

How Adults Learn

Being a good speaker isn't always about what you say but HOW you deliver the information. When presenting on stage or in video, you are also in the entertainment and storytelling business. The more the audience can relate to your stories, the more they will enjoy your presentation, and the more they will gain from your teachings.

We can break down the level of involvement for the audience into passive and active. This is called the *Learning Pyramid*. Now there is a lot of controversy about the leaning pyramid and if these percentages are 100% accurate, but forget the actual percentages and compare the activities to how you actually learn and which activities would keep you engaged during a long workshop or speech.

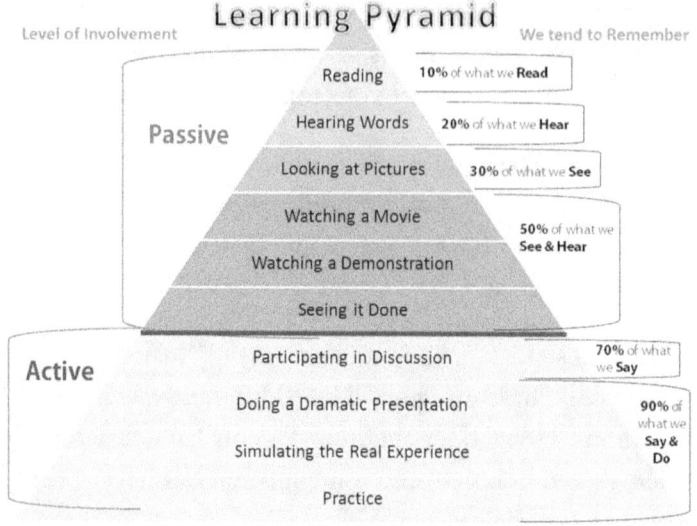

Confucius: I hear and forget, I see and remember, I do and I understand

The top of the pyramid is considered passive involvement which means the audience doesn't do much but sit down, look, and listen. The least amount of retention for the audience is at the top of the pyramid, then as the pyramid expands the amount of retention will increase based on the level of involvement from the audience. When delivering a presentation you want your audience to be involved in as many of these activities as possible.

Do you remember sitting down in a classroom and listening for a teacher for an hour only to be completely bored and using all your energy to avoid falling asleep? As adults, the same thing can happen if we take a traditional school teacher approach for delivering a speech. Always remember when writing your content, you are in the entertainment and storytelling business when you are presenting anything type of material to any audience.

In the passive section you can achieve these six behaviors by using handouts, using a PowerPoint presentation as a visual aid, and a short video clip.

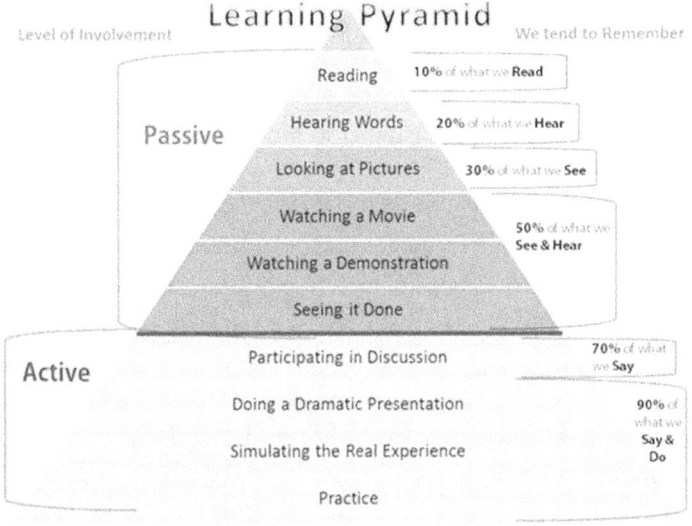

In the active area you have to get more creative but it is possible to keep the audience active while sitting there watching you deliver your speech. After you teach a couple of important pieces of content, than ask the audience to get into small groups of 4 or 5, and then give them questions to discuss within the group. By showing how something needs to get done you can ask a few volunteers from the audience and do a dramatic presentation to simulate a real experience. Lastly, you can give the audience a chance to practice a skill in their small groups.

> **"** I hear and forget, I
> see and remember, I do
> and understand. *–Confucius*

To support both the passive and active learning there are three main types of learning styles that apply to most anyone. Those are auditory, visual, and kinesthetic.

Auditory learning is those types of people that learn from hearing others talk. They can learn through a lecture, group discussion, audio such as podcasts, books on tape, and Q & A sessions where the learner can hear from others in addition to the facilitator.

Visual learners learn by seeing PowerPoint slides, charts, flipcharts, reading/uncovering information in a book, digital photos, videos or video podcasts, online training, and handouts.

The last group of learners is kinesthetic. These types of learners like to practice hands-on so use things such as simulations, role plays, and group activities.

Spend time as needed on the various items above to ensure they are comfortable building their sessions around this knowledge to become more effective. When you combine all three of these areas then you can rest assured everyone in the audience is learning.

10 Different Ways to Build the Audience Excitement

Even though I have said it a few times, I don't think I could ever say it enough; you are in the entertainment and storytelling business when you are a public speaker or conducting a presentation for a group of people.

Your main purpose for any speech is to teach your audience something of importance that they can apply to improve their personal life, business, or career. Learning should be fun so that the crowd will stay engaged and pay attention. Here are a few ideas that will help you to create an "entertainment" style speech and so you can also tie in all those behaviors we discussed in the Learning Pyramid.

1. Making an Entrance

How you begin your stage presence will get the audience excited about listening to you or cause them to immediately take a bathroom break. There are many different ways to do this; of course, these will depend on your audience and your teaching topic. You can select one of these ideas or get creative and come up with your own.

On Stage

- Do you have a theme song that you will always enter the stage with? This is a great branding tool if you market yourself as a speaker.

- You can show a short video clip that will build curiosity about what you are going to share with the audience.

- Come out dancing, jumping up and down clapping to a great tune that the audience will love and just can't sit still. You may be saying to yourself, 'no way would I ever have the guts to do this', yet enthusiasm is contagious and your audience will never be able to reach your level of energy so you MUST have very high energy in your physical behavior or in your voice and facial expressions.

- Walk onto the stage and shake the hand of the person that introduced you or hug them. Then immediately crack a joke about an experience with the person that introduced you if you know them personally. If you don't know them personally then you can crack a joke about traveling to your location or the city you are speaking.

On Video

- Create a short video introduction that plays catchy music. You can find someone to create one for you on Fiverr.

- Whiteboard introductions are a big thing now and you can have your motto or mission statement shown in this type of video. Again, Fiverr.com is a great resource.

2. Opening Statement.

Your opening statement will set the stage for your success and allow your personality to shine through while grabbing the audience's attention at the same time. You have about 90 seconds to get them engaged in your presentation so use that time wisely.

- Attention Getter. This is telling a personal story that your audience is craving to know more and to get to the end. It is very descriptive and builds a picture in the audience's mind. You want to get their imagination working. This personal story can be a lesson you learned that applies to your teaching.
- What's In It For Them (WIIFM). We are all selfish and if you say you aren't then you are kidding yourself. We all want to know what we will gain from a presentation. How will it help me lose weight, how will it help my business increase its profits, and how will it help me get my next promotion? The WIIFM is a promise of what the audience will gain if they pay

attention, take notes, and apply your strategies to a particular area in their life, business, or career.

- Powerful Quote. Everyone loves quotes. Have you been on Facebook and Twitter? Quotes are motivating and they are typically the images that get more attention on social media. So why couldn't it work in a presentation too? Obviously you can't use a random quote, be sure and use one that applies to your content.

- Video Clip. You want a video clip to be under 2 minutes with music and a message behind it. The video needs to entice an emotion: happy, sad, excited, laughter, etc. When I was conducting customer service training for a restaurant I had a video clip that showed different horrible dining experiences from famous movies and TV shows. It was a big hit and it set the stage that we are talking about how to take great care of our restaurant customers.

- Unusual Information or Statistics. People are amazed by numbers and things that the normal person doesn't know about. The information and statistic should apply to your content and the audience's world.

3. Icebreaker.

An activity or role-play is something the audience will participate in that helps them relax with the people around them. These are a necessity if you plan on breaking your audience into small groups, and you expect them to share information with strangers. An icebreaker may be a quiz that the group takes, a personal story they share with their group, or you give them a task or challenge. There are many books on the market with great ideas for icebreakers, just google 'meeting icebreakers'.

4. Storytelling.

You want to include personal stories or scenario stories that help get your points across to the audience. These help your audience connect with you and they will feel like they know you even though you have never met them before. People love to hear about other people's struggles, success, and embarrassing moments so be sure and tie those into your material.

5. Using Visual Aids and Handouts.

Visual aids and handouts is any material that the audience can look at while you are speaking or they have in their hands during your presentation and can take home. These add a lot of value to your audience as they can take notes and can always refer back to their material after your presentation. I keep all my workbooks and handouts from presentations that I felt were valuable in my life and career. If you sell your own content online it is also a great reminder for previous attendees to go back to your website and possible purchase more of your products.

6. Ask for Volunteers.

One of the most effective and hilarious presentations I saw was when the speaker asked for specific volunteers from the audience and she did a role play. Of course, the volunteer had no idea what was going to happen which made it so much fun for the rest of the audience. The speaker was able to communicate her point through the actions of the volunteer and it was awesome. Her point was how men would respond in a particular situation with their wife. Of course it was her area of expertise so she as the presenter was prepared to respond based on his reaction. If you choose to do this then you must be prepared for any crazy reaction from the volunteer if you are trying to teach a certain lesson.

7. Build Teamwork and Support.

Anytime you can get the entire audience doing something at the same time it really brings energy. Doing anything where they feel a part of it gets a great response. One speaker I saw at a conference was teaching the power of thinking positively and how negative thoughts hold you back. After his motivating speech, he asked for 3 volunteers to come up on stage and each of them was going to break a board in front of hundreds of people. The speaker knowing the volunteers would be nervous and need a lot of support, he insisted that every person in the room get up out of their seat and surround the stage shouting "do it, do it, do it, do it". Every person on stage broke the board, and it was a fun, exciting experience for everyone involved.

8. Involve Social Media.

A great way to get the entire audience participating is to create a unique hashtag to your presentation. You can encourage the audience to tweet throughout your presentation some great a-ha points and you can tweet during the breaks or have someone on your staff tweeting throughout your presentation. This will not only get your audience engaged but you may book some additional speaking opportunities from the additional attention. It can also drive more traffic to your website for others that are not in attendance.

Whether you are on stage or conducting a live stream training online, be sure it is being recorded. You want to place your training in different locations on social media: You Tube, Google +, Twitter, Pinterest, etc. The more locations you can post your training the more website traffic you will receive.

9. Plan Adequate Breaks.

A break for the body and the mind is a must. If you are conducting a long workshop then you need to schedule a 15 minute break every hour or ninety minutes. The longer someone sits down without movement will cause them to feel irritated or slip into a mind coma.

Allowing them to go to the bathroom, stretch their legs, and get their blood pumping will bring their minds back fresh when they enter the workshop. It also gives the audience a chance to network which is a benefit of any gathering.

Even if you are doing a live stream video, you must have breaks. You would treat this just as you would if the participants were live. Give them the time that you have and then tell them the exact time that you will be back on line so they can get up and walk around too. Make sure you have a still photo with the name of your training showing during the break. The best way is to show a countdown clock so everyone knows exactly when you will start the training session again.

10. Call to Action.

For the audience to gain the most of your teaching, you want to direct them on the next steps. Many times people can get overwhelmed with too much information so you need to break it down into two or three challenges or steps they need to do after leaving your presentation. This helps your purpose of ensuring the audience can apply your teachings to their life, business, or career. When they positive results from your teaching, they will visit your website and possibly purchase additional products.

11. Closing Statement.

Your closing statement is the last sentences and thoughts you will leave with the audience. So make them good! You can choose from the same strategies as you used in the opening statement: WIIFM, personal story, powerful quote, etc. There is one difference with the closing statement and that it must tie everything together. It is like tying your presentation up with a bow and not leaving anything left for the audience to wonder about or want to ask questions about.

A best practice is to tie the closing statement in with your opening statement. When done correctly it adds a sense of completion, and is a very natural way to provide closure.

You never want to give new information in the conclusion. If you add new points then the audience will not have a sense of closure. Even though you don't want to add new points you can certainly review any relevant points you already discussed.

Always end strong or your audience will be left with a less then positive impression. Standing there saying, "That's it" does not make a lasting impression with your audience.

Chapter 4
Equipment & Room Set-Up

The audience is likely to remember
only three things from your
presentation or speech.
~Stephen Keague

Presentation Types

We already defined public speaking as being more than a keynote speaker on the big stage. Public speaking is when you address a group of people no matter how small, and you are put on the spot with all eyes in the room listening and watching how you present yourself! There are many different types of presentations that require public speaking. To be able to provide the best experience for your audience, you need to know what type of presentation you are delivering.

Once you have the type of presentation then you can determine the presentation style and amount of interactivity which may be possible. Doing a keynote presentation for thousands of people is far different than talking to a group of 23 sitting at a U-shaped table. The delivery style required is much different for each presentation type and must be delivered effectively to both groups. Here are a few basic ideas for interactivity based on the type of presentation being delivered:

Keynotes

A keynote speaker presents to larger groups and is often thought of as a speech. Keynote presentations typically command the room and the speaker is the focus of the presentation. The main focus is often getting information delivered to a group with little time for group exercises or skill validation.

Getting audience involvement may include exercises such as getting the group up to stretch, greeting as many people as you can in 15 seconds, creating some sort of motivational exercise, group interaction or having them 'vote' with a show of hands.

This type of presentation has the least amount of audience participation.

Workshop/Seminar

These are typically in smaller groups and more time is spent on role playing and skill building exercises. These presentations typically involve some presentation from the stage, and then hands-on practice of the content taught.

These types of presentations are usually used within specific industry conferences.

Round Table Discussions

Round tables are great ways to have people break into smaller groups and focus on a number of tasks by rotating from one table to the next. At each table, there is a specific topic to be discussed in the group and then all the notes are gathered and then emailed to all the participants a few days later. Presenting in this format is more of a moderator role by ensuring the directions and expected outcomes are clearly communicated. The presenter basically gives instructions, and will then keep time so the groups will know when to rotate to their next table.

Team-Building Exercises

Overseeing team building exercises is a form of presentation and is also considered a facilitator role. Directions need to be clearly given. Quite often items must be purchased in advance and setup/organized for the session to be effective.

Live Stream Training

This is where you can set up your equipment and present in a room or on a stage while being streamed live on the internet through video. There can be some technical difficulties, but you can deliver a great stage-like presentation and reach people all over the world. You can also offer a live chat during your presentation so the attendees can ask questions and a member of your staff is answering them or feeding them to you to answer throughout the presentation.

Once you know the presentation type, then you need to know the number of people attending so you can plan your room configuration for tables, chairs, your stage, handouts, etc.

Room Configuration

Obviously the room configuration will not be important for live stream, but it is for in person presentations. For the right table configuration, you will need to know the number of attendees and if you will be on stage. A stage is typically needed for groups over 100 so they can see you. YOU need to be the center of the group's attention so plan accordingly and position yourself (and the A/V) in the right spot.

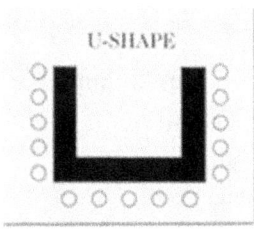

U-Shape: Great for the audience to be able to interact with each other, good for team building and for the presenter to interact with each audience member because of the openness. Yet be careful as you pace / turn so the group doesn't see your back too much.

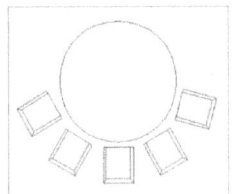

Crescent Rounds: These are good for interaction as people can see those at their table and nobody has their back to the stage (as compared to full round seating). They work well if you have a lot of different activities where they larger group needs to breakdown to a smaller one. This way they groups are already defined.

Full Rounds: Used for 'roundtable discussions' and meals but the downside is that many people have their back to the presenter.

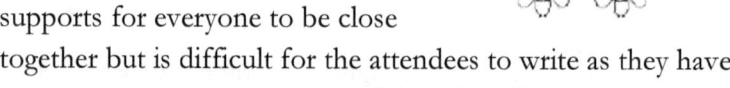

Theater: This style of seating supports for everyone to be close together but is difficult for the attendees to write as they have

no solid surface. Often this is the only option with large groups. You need to know in advance if this will be the setup as it may limit your ability to have the audience move around.

Classroom: This is a typical setup of chairs with a thin table in front of each person. Nice writing surface and pretty informal. Setting the tables at an angle is called a 'herringbone' and can add a little variety.

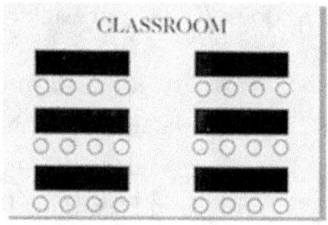

Conference Style: Good for informal presentations or small groups where much discussion will take place. If using a projector, remove the 'head of the table' seat so everyone has a clear view.

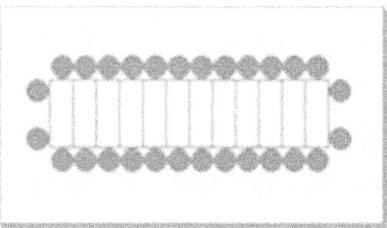

Audio Visual

We are going to cover just the basics for planning your audio visual needs. This section is really important because it will affect how effective your speech will be. If there is too much lighting on the stage, then the audience may not be able to see your PowerPoint presentation because of a glare.

Lighting

For in person presentation you need to look at how is the room lit? Fluorescent bulbs which are only off or on? Dimmer switches? Is there a chandelier right in front of the screen? Know these things in advance, as well as how to control and adjust them. If you are going to show a video clip, then you need to have the main lights over the audience dimmed so they can see the screen without a glare.

For live streaming or google hangouts on air, you need to check the lighting on your face. You don't want to have any dark shadows or make it difficult for the participants to see your face. You want to try and create the same interaction as if the participants were sitting in front of you.

Internet Connection

For in person and live streaming, the strength of the internet connection is very important. Believe it or not, you have to ask if the connection works. When dealing with any technology you MUST test everything first and also have a back-up plan. You need to plan for the worst scenario. If you are teaching a workshop and a bad storm knocked out the internet, what would you do? You want to maintain your professionalism at all times in front of a group so even though there are small chances that things may happen, you still must have a Plan B.

Music

Music is a huge part of setting the mood of a presentation. You want to have music playing as you participants hop on live stream training or when your audience enters the room. You also want to include music playing during breaks. You don't want to have silence during those times. Be sure and keep the mood upbeat.

Microphone

You will want to use a microphone for groups over 40 or if you do not have a commanding voice. Avoid using a podium unless you are introducing a speaker or accepting an award. By not using a podium during a presentation you are able to move around on the stage which helps keep your audience engaged.

When possible use a wireless lavaliere which allows your hands to be free for those proper hand gestures. Always have a backup microphone just in case your lavaliere battery dies or it breaks.

Laptop

When you are using a PowerPoint presentation you will want to place the file on your desktop so you can easily find it. Be sure and clean up your desktop icons so it doesn't look cluttered and turn off all screen savers and hibernate off so your laptop doesn't shut down in the middle of your presentation. How embarrassing!

As your Plan B, have your presentation on a jump drive also. Sometimes when you are speaking at an event that has multiple speakers they will want your presentation on their computer so they can arrange all the slides in the correct order of the speakers.

I can't say this enough, but if you are using your laptop test it out and don't forget your charger. I did that one time and the battery ran out on my laptop and my presentation went black. This is probably one of my most embarrassing teaching moments.

LCD Projector

Projectors can cause problems like any other piece of technology. One thing you need to have with you is a backup bulb for the projector. You don't have a warning on when the bulbs will go out, and yes they can be pricey but isn't it worth it to save your expertise image.

Visual Aids

Visual aids are a great way to get your point across and it gives the audience something to look at and take home to review at a later time. You can reinforce your message visually by the use of graphs, handouts, and flipcharts.

Flipchart

Now you don't see people use flipcharts a lot as these are considered "old school" but they still have their place in a presentation environment. If there is one thing a flipchart is good for and that is a 'parking lot'. The 'parking lot' is used when someone asks a question that is off-topic and you want to come back and answer it so you can stay on your current subject. When you do this you won't forget to address a question before ending the presentation.

Flipcharts are great when used properly and completely annoying for the audience when used incorrectly, so here are a few checkpoints to remember.

- Use with a small audience – 20 or fewer people
- When writing, stand at an angle so your back is never to the audience
- Write neat and use bright colors and big letters! *[Mr. Sketch markers work really well. A good rule of thumb is 1" tall for every 15 feet of classroom]*
- Use post-it flipchart paper or tape to post on walls
- Keep it legible

- Pre-write some flipchart pages to keep the presentation moving

Handouts / Downloads

Handouts are great to support the material you are teaching and can provide take home value for the attendee. You want to give out handouts prior to the start of your presentation. You don't want to stop teaching to hand them out. So with internet training session, you want to deliver the download to the participants prior to joining the live stream training. You want to make the most of the time you have in front of your audience. Since people remember very little of what you say, providing a participant guide or handout gives them something to refer back to at a later date.

There are different types of handouts you can provide for your audience:

- Binder that includes the participant guide. This would be used for a conference that is multiple days.
- Call to Action Card. This can be any size, laminated and colorful that includes your website, presentation headline, the key points of your presentation and their next steps or call to action after they leave the workshop.
- Stapled Multi-page handout. Maybe you only have a couple of pages that you feel is a must-have for your audience, and then just staple the handout.

- PowerPoint Handouts: Building a presentation one time in PowerPoint and using some of the features, enables you to print leader's guides and handouts by using the notes feature when printing.
- Download: Offer a link in an email or on a website to the pdf and have the audiences download and print it themselves.

There are many different ways to leave something behind with your audience, just provide them with the most important information. Never feel obligated to give them everything you are teaching.

PowerPoint

PowerPoint has taken over presentations with one speaker trying to out-do another. However, people are so sick of seeing bad slide shows, presenters must be careful.

PowerPoint can be a great enhancement to your presentation without being the presentation. The biggest mistake trainers make in this area is using PPT as a crutch or teleprompter. Instead of memorizing the presentation and rehearsing, too many presenters simply fly in one point at a time and read off the slides to the group. Two words for that type of presentation – BO-RING! The purpose of the PowerPoint is to help keep you on track for the correct order of your material, to keep the presentation flowing smoothly, and to give the most important key points for the audience to see visually.

PowerPoint is very simple to use when you set up the master slides. You can set it up one time properly so each slide type will be consistent. The setting up the background, you want to use light colored font on dark backgrounds and dark colored fonts on light backgrounds. You want to keep the colors minimal and consistent with your company or brand. There are other best practices that you want to follow when using PowerPoint and setting up your master slide.

Font

- Lose the animations/fly-ins. If you want to use animation use the simple fade in and use the same animation throughout the presentation. When you have a lot of different types of animation it becomes distracting for the audience.

- Don't use sounds with text.

- Don't use fonts that are unique or not standard on all computers. When using another PC to present, your presentation will not look the same because it will not have the unique font uploaded. It is always best to use standard fonts like Times New Roman, Georgia, Arial, and Verdana. Also, use two different types of fonts at the most. Use one font for the slide title and another font for the body.

- Font size should be 22 point at a minimum if you have to otherwise 28 point is the smallest size. Keep the key points on the slide simple. You don't have to write in complete sentences because it is only a bullet point that you will explain in detail.

Slide Layout

- Avoid more than 6 lines and 6 words per line on each slide.

- Use more visual images. It's more eye appealing to the audience, conveys the message quickly.

Images

Be sure to use pictures that are adequate size and clarity. Pictures can be distracting when they include information that is not relevant.

When using a picture, allow yourself adequate time to explain what it represents so that your audience can digest its message. Keeping a picture up for too long a period of time will cause it to be distracting, especially during live stream or recorded videos. Likewise, taking it away from an audience's view before they are ready will create a confusion point and distract from your message. Usually, 10 seconds is adequate for an audience to digest a picture. You can speak about the picture during this time, and can also be silent for a few seconds so that your audience can appreciate the image you have given them.

When using images be sure that you give credit to the source. You don't want to get into legal trouble by borrowing an image that is copyrighted. You can purchase stock images and pay a small fee or the best way is to use your own images.

Diagrams, charts, or graphs

Certain numbers, information, and statistics need added clarity. You can deliver this by providing a graph, chart, or diagram could be a way to clarify complicated numbers, concepts, or comparisons for your audience. Anytime you create a diagram, chart, or graph, it will be displayed most professionally on a PowerPoint slide. You can also include diagrams and charts on your handout material.

When creating a chart, aim for clarity in the ideas that you want to present. It is easy to create charts that show too much information for your audience to digest. You want to keep it simple and have the graph or chart represent the most important content. Even though some of the information is relevant to your topic, using too much will cause your audience to tune out the visual aid and disregard its content. Be very careful to choose only the most essential information to display in a chart or graph, and leave the rest out. In other words, simplify information so that your message is clear cut and not cluttered.

Media Resources

<u>Film or audio clips</u>

With social media, Skype, smart phones, Google Hangout on Air, You Tube, etc. today's generation continues to raise the bar on expectations. You want to keep up with the times and use the technology that everyone is using when possible. If you walked in with a VHS of a video clip that you want to play during your presentation, it is likely that they wouldn't even have the correct equipment to play the VHS video. Not only did VHS dead but do are CDs and DVDs are on the way out!

With the variety and accessibility of just about any topic on YouTube; it is just a click away to find clips from your favorite movie, TV show, or another industry expert. These clips can be a great visual aid to help illustrate a particular aspect of your speech. However, when not used properly they can also be very distracting.

When using a film or audio clip, always check all the software and hardware you will be using beforehand. Check to make sure the volume is at an appropriate level, for example, and that your clip is going to start in the right spot. Not doing a pre-speech check could easily result in you fumbling around during your speech, talking to yourself or absentmindedly to your audience, and create a huge distraction point in your speech.

Here are some tips on how to use certain media sources properly:

- Videos should fit seamlessly into your presentation from both a speaking standpoint. Rehearsal is the key to make sure everything works properly.

- Videos/DVDs – playing a video clip can help 'tell a story' to illustrate a key point

- Embed the clips in the PPT or use a DVD player outside the presentation

- Appropriate Length of clip – Keep it around 1-2 minutes or break it up into smaller parts.

- Copyright Issues – You will need permission to reprint articles, newsletters, DVDs, videos, etc. to provide/show to groups.

Remember, media, just like visual aids and is intended to highlight key points and reinforce your message, not become the message.

Room Setup

On the day of your event, you want to follow up with all the details of the room set up. You do not want to trust others with the details of your presentation because you will be the one embarrassed if any of these areas aren't ready to the audience's satisfaction.

Here is a checklist to help you focus on the most important details.

Number of Attendees

- Are their enough seats?
- Can they all see you?

Name Badges

- Ensure these are setup in advance and names are spelled correctly
- If you are planning a team exercise, perhaps having a color-coded sticker on the nametag would encourage interaction (this works well when using the Theatre seating style since they aren't broken down by groups at tables)

Visual Aids

- Where will the audience receive their handouts? Are they left on their chairs? Are they on a table as they enter? Will there be people handing them out before the presentation?
- Are there enough copies for the number of attendees?

Branding

- Ensure the room and tables are branded: company colors, balloons, trinkets/giveaways, banners, etc.
- If you don't brand the room because you are a speaker for an organization, always be sure your handouts and all materials are branded with your information.

Stage/Screen

- Get comfortable with the logistics of the room. Are there any places you can't walk?
- Should you stay on stage?
- Can everyone see you?

Audio/Visual & Music

- Where is the projector located?
- Are there any cords I need to be aware of when walking on stage or around the room?
- Do I have a 'clicker' for my PowerPoint presentation and backup batteries?
- Where do I get my microphone and where is the emergency backup?

- Where are the speakers for the music? Test the volume of the music before allowing people to enter the room. Is the music loaded and in correct order that you want it played?

Temperature

- Ensure the temperature is just right. Too hot or cold and you are no longer the center of attention!

Refreshments

- Are you setting them up and are they ready?
- Do you have all the supplies: ice, cups, or maybe a soda cooler?
- Inside or outside the room?

Promo Material

- If you are a paid speaker and you have additional tools and resources to sell, where will the sales table be set up?

Chapter 5

Preparing the Content

The success of your presentation will be judged not by the knowledge you send but by what the listener receives.
~Lilly Walters

Structure of Your Presentation

Every presentation has similar structure so placing the correct content in order is simple. There are three main sections: Introduction, Body, and Conclusion. There are three main areas to create for each main section of your presentation.

Introduction	Body of Presentation	Conclusion
Part 1: Welcome	Part 4: Three Main Objectives	Part 7: Call to Action
Part 2: Opening Statement	Part 5: Key Teaching Points	Part 8: Review Objectives
Part 3: Purpose or Goal	Part 6: Activities / Role-Plays	Part 9: Closing Statement

Introduction

Part 1: Welcome

The introduction is the time that you start building rapport with your audience and establishing credibility. Always thank the audience and/or the organization you are addressing. You want to show your enthusiasm and appreciate from the beginning. Your audience will immediately watch how you act and begin to feed off your energy or lack of energy.

Giving a little background about yourself will help them connect with you on a personal level, and you will also build credibility for the topic you are going to teach. You want to give the audience a reason to stick around, and not take a bathroom break during your presentation.

This is the time you could add an icebreaker to help the audience to relax, and get them engaged in the beginning. We discussed examples of these in a previous chapter.

Part 2: Strong Opening Statement

We discussed this in quite some detail in Chapter 2 just remember this is the time to entertain your audience with a captivating story, quote, or scenario that introduces your speech topic. It needs to capture their attention within 90 seconds.

It needs to be a strong statement and a promise of what the audience will gain by taking the time to listen. The bigger the benefits, the longer your audience still stay engaged and the benefit determines the level of their participation.

Part 3: Purpose / Goal and Why

Every presentation must have clear objectives and a clear purpose. You want to state exactly what the audience is going to learn from your presentation. By doing this you are setting clear expectations on what the audience should expect so the entire room is on the same page.

You want to have one purpose or also called 'end in mind' for the audience. This means if there is one skill set or one goal you want the audience to take home with them what would it be?

When you are explaining to your audience about your goal and objectives you must always include the reasons 'why' this goal is important. This can help to open up the minds of skeptics when hearing the purpose for the first time, and it applies to WIIFM [What's In It For Me]. Your audience will listen as long as they are clear on the benefits for them and what they will gain.

You will be tempted to include a lot of goals but choose ONLY one! Next you will give them detailed information to learn more through the three main objectives that support the one goal.

Guidelines for a proper goal statement:

- Write the goal as a complete sentence, phrased as a statement, not a question. It should include a promise that you will deliver to the audience.
- It needs to be clear and concise so the audience knows exactly what you plan on delivering in your speech.
- It should address one big idea.
- The goal needs to apply to the audience's needs for their life, business, or career.

Body of Presentation

Part 4: Two to Three Main Objectives

The rule of thumb is you only have a maximum of 3 objectives to teach, and a minimum of two objectives that support the overall purpose of your presentation.

You may think that only three main points isn't enough information but anything more than that and people will not remember. When you are conducting a presentation you don't want your audience to be overwhelmed by giving them too much information. You deliver value when your participants are able to walk out with one or two great ideas they can immediately put into practice for their life, business, or career.

Also, people have a tendency to think in three's.

Breakfast, Lunch, Dinner

Past, Present, Future

Reading, Writing, Arithmetic

Morning, Afternoon, Night

Kids say, "I learned my A-B-C's"

Have you ever heard, "It's easy as 1-2-3"?

For example, if I am going to teach a workshop for restaurant managers on how to run a profitable restaurant here is my overall purpose/goal and my 3 objectives to support the goal.

Goal: For restaurant managers to effective manage the highest expenses in the restaurant, food cost.

Objectives:

1. Understand how to calculate an accurate food cost analysis.
2. Know the best practices of how to conduct a consistent inventory each week.
3. Learn negotiation tactics to get the best quality food ingredients for the best available cost.

These objectives are basically the agenda for the entire presentation. So how do you begin to figure out the top three objectives for your purpose? You may want to make a big list of all the things you feel are important about your goal, and then begin to see which details are main headings and which ones are supportive ideas for the main headings.

Part 5: Key Teaching Points

The body of the presentation is the details that supports the three objectives. So let me go back to my restaurant manager example and show you bullets or supportive ideas underneath the three objectives.

Goal: For restaurant managers to effective manage the highest expenses in the restaurant, food cost.

[objective #1] Understand how to calculate an accurate food cost analysis.

[body] Teach the exact formula for a food cost analysis.

[body] Share the correct range for food cost.

[body] Best practices for ordering product so to not over-order and not run out of product until the next delivery day.

[objective #2] Know the best practices of how to conduct a consistent inventory each week.

[body] Step by step process of how to conduct inventory.

[body] The number of people needed and their exact roles.

[body] Troubleshooting steps when food cost is too high or too low.

[objective #3] Learn negotiation tactics to get the best quality food ingredients for the best available cost.

[body] How to find different vendors.

[body] Contract prices vs. no contract.

[body] Steps to be aware of product prices increases during specific seasons.

You can see that I still kept to the three rules even with the bullet points that will build the body portion. There is a lot that can be covered when talking about food cost for a restaurant so these key points do not cover everything but remember the goal is to teach your audience one or two new things. You will never be able to cover everything about the topic you are teaching. So build your speech or presentation around the biggest needs of improvement for the audience.

What problems keep them up at night? What solutions have they been searching for and haven't found? Focus on the biggest needs of your audience and you will have a winner.

As an extra in these teaching points, you must include a success story or proof of success. What evidence do you have that can support the points you are teaching? There has to be motivation why someone would want to put into practice the things you are teaching them, and you must have evidence that what you are teaching them is the truth and that it worked for others.

Part 6: Activities / Role Plays

After you have written your objectives and the three main teaching points for each, then review those and see which ones would need an activity or a role-play. You will need these placed in the correct area of your presentation so when you teach a skill set then you give the audience a chance to put the kill into practice.

For example, if I was teaching 'public speaking' as a workshop then after I taught the audience how to select a goal and the objectives, then I would give them a chance to select a topic and write a goal with the objectives and body speaking points. Or after I taught the group about body language then I would break them up into small groups and have them practice a small presentation in front of the group to practice proper body language and facial expressions. You want to teach them something, and then immediately begin to apply it through an activity or role-play.

The above two examples are perfect examples of a role-play, but that isn't always the best choice. Sometimes you just want them to participate in an activity. An activity is different than a role-play because it causes the participant to think through decisions that must be made and/or work together with a team. Here are some examples of activities that you may use:

Pre-Quiz or Post-Quiz: Starting a presentation with a pre-quiz will show the participant how much about a subject they still don't understand and still need to learn. A post-quiz is also given so they can see the difference in their scores directly after your presentation. This helps the audience to see how much the learned during your presentation.

Problem-Solving: The group can be divided into smaller groups or it can be used as an individual activity. Give a couple different scenarios, and then they must decide how to handle the problem using a technique just taught.

Brainstorming: Divide the group into smaller groups, and have them brainstorm a certain subject with ways to solve a problem. Then after the brainstorm session, have a speaker for each group to share their ideas with the entire room.

Conclusion

Part 7: Call to Action / Next Steps

When you deliver great information, the audience isn't in a place to immediately figure out how to apply your tips to their life, business, or career. So you need to help them to take the right path; otherwise, they may walk out and never apply anything you taught. This is why you need a 'call to action' or 'next steps'. This gives them a breakdown of what they need to do to apply your valuable information.

To wrap up the restaurant manager scenario, here would be some action steps:

1. Analyze your delivery schedule; do you need more delivery days or less?

2. Select the two people to conduct inventory every week and assign roles for each.

3. Review any food contracts you currently have for your restaurant, and research to find out if you have the best prices.

4. Monitor par levels on a daily basis and follow a product mix report.

I only gave four action steps but you can have more or less. Heck, you can have only one! I do recommend you don't go overboard on the action steps and choose the most important ones that will help them get results faster. If the list is too long, many participants will think it takes too much work and do nothing. Remember, they have busy lives so they need to believe it is doable with their business schedule.

Part 8: Review Objectives

When you have finished presenting all your material and have discussed the audience's action steps, then review the original objectives. You want to take about 5 minutes and include a review of what you promised with your one goal/purpose and the three objectives they should gain from the your presentation.

This helps the audience remember all the main points they should learn and it shows them that you followed through on your promise.

Part 9: Closing Statement

Your closing statement is the last thing you will say to the audience before exiting the stage or ending a video or live stream training. Again, this is another area we discussed in detail previously but to recap there are three things you must remember during your closing statement.

1. Never introduce a new topic.

2. Always bring the presentation to a close by tying your close in with your opening statement.

3. Always thank the audience for their participation and for allowing you to spend time with them.

Creating a Presentation Outline

When you need to write a presentation, you need to have the skeleton outline completed first before you begin writing your presentation in paragraph form. When you take the extra time in the beginning to organize your thoughts and place the topics in the correct order, then you will spend less time making corrections in the end. When you do not organize your topics and place them in an outline first, then it will become difficult to edit your presentation. Many of your important teaching points will get forgotten, and not placed in your presentation.

Below is a basic outline format for your first presentation. It includes the nine main sections we just covered in detail. So let's put what we learned into practice and in the space provided, fill in your main bullet points you want to cover. Be sure you write them out in complete sentence format.

Introduction

Part 1: Welcome

Part 2: Strong Opening Statement

Part 3: Main Purpose / Goal

Part 4: 3 Main Objectives

    1.

    2.

    3.

Body of Presentation

Objective #1 *(You don't have to have three teaching points and one proof, I just included extra space)*

    Teaching Point

    Teaching Point

    Teaching Point

Success Story / Proof

Objective #2

Teaching Point

Teaching Point

Teaching Point

Success Story / Proof

Objective #3 (Optional)

Teaching Point

Teaching Point

Teaching Point

Success Story / Proof

Part 6: Activities / Role-Plays

Part 7: Call to Action / Next Steps

Part 8: Review Goal & Objectives

Part 9: Closing Statement

Researching Your Topic

Now that you have the main ideas of your presentation outlined, you need to do some research for your topic. You will use this information to build the content of your speech and add credibility to what you say.

Options for Reference Material

Even though you may be an expert on your topic, you want to do research to add to your presentation. Get the world's perspective on your subject, or find some mind-blowing statistic to share with the audience. There are a ton of resources especially with social media and the internet. The following are options you can use for reference material in your speech:

- Newspaper
- Magazine
- Internet
- TV or Radio Production
- Published Book
- Interviewing other Experts
- You Tube videos
- Google Hangouts

Internet Search Engines

When searching for material to use in your presentation, a good place to start is an internet search engine such as

'Google'. Be sure to use proper searching techniques such as including the words "and" or "not" in order to narrow your search properly. Other searching tips are to use quotation marks (" ") around phrases that belong together such as "American baseball" so that your search doesn't produce results that contain only one of those words individually. Finally, limit the use of filler words like the, and, in, etc. For example, if you were to do a search for how to do proper abdominal crunches, don't type in: How a person can do proper abdominal crunches. Instead, typing in the line: proper "abdominal crunches" should return better results. Notice 45 putting the quotation marks around the words "abdominal crunches" so that the search engine result is specific to the term you are interested in.

Research Worksheet

Before you begin researching your topic, it is a good idea to be clear on what you are searching for. If you do not, then it will increase your research time and you could get your presentation completely off track from what you want to accomplish. Below are a few questions you can answer prior to beginning your research.

1.   My subject area is:

     _____

2.   My topic is: _____

3.   The main things that I already know about this topic are:

     _____

     _____

4. I am already aware of the following good resources on this topic:

_____

_____

5. Three questions that I need to research about my topic are:

a. _____

b. _____

c. _____

6. Three good search terms or search phrases to use while searching the Internet are:

a. _____ b. _____ c. _____

9. A good person to interview in order to learn more about this topic is: _____

10. Three good interview questions about this topic are:

a. _____

b. _____

c. _____

Manuscript

After you have the presentation outline completed, you will need to write out your full content which is a manuscript of your presentation. It is important to write the manuscript out as close to your normal talking points so you have an accurate idea of how long your presentation will last. The idea is not to memorize this word for word, but rather to have a script worked out to help you review the flow of your presentation. You would never want to read a manuscript outline for a public speech. The following are guidelines for the manuscript:

- Write out your presentation as if you were talking. Be sure it is written where is sounds natural.
- Use your manuscript to time out how long your presentation will most likely last, and to get a sense of the overall tone your speech should have.
- Never read your manuscript during the actual speech, no matter how tempting it is to have the polished wording spoken.

Chapter 6
Prepare Yourself

Practice does not make perfect. Only perfect practice makes perfect.
~Vince Lombardi

Steps to Practice Perfectly

Now that we have covered how to prepare your content, the next step is preparing yourself to present your material to a group. We shared many different ways to calm your nerves and rehearsing is the most important. Many people 'rehearse' but don't practice properly and end up with a sub-par performance.

One thing to remember is that even the pros practice. Sports teams practice their same plays over and over again. Actors and musicians practice scenes or songs multiple times. Develop the same mentality with your presentation skills! Practice until you get it right every time. To perfect your presentation you must practice correctly, so here are a few points to put into practice.

First, **memorize the flow of the material.** You will want to keep your eyes on the audience, and not the PowerPoint slides or the teleprompter. If you are conducting live stream training, then you want your eyes on the camera at all times or on the webcam for a Google Hangout. Nothing turns participants off more to see someone read their speech off a screen, piece of paper, or read bullet points directly from a slide. To avoid being dependent on your tools you must practice multiple times. Practicing over and over will help you memorize the flow of the information which in return will enhance your credibility with the audience.

If you need a little crutch you can use note cards to refer back to but don't get in the habit of reading from them. If you are using PowerPoint, know what you are going to say about each slide but use the slides as a prompt/reminder for you and a visual medium for the audience. Don't simply read the text or use the slide as your notes.

Once you commit to memory the flow of your presentation, then you need to **Time It.** It is really important that you are able to time your presentation correctly because most conferences are on a tight timeline and you want to make sure you can get all your valuable information within the correct time without rushing and leaving anything out. Time your presentation by speaking out loud as you would during the presentation. Use all your training tools such as handouts and PowerPoint slides just as you would if you were in front of the group. Then you want to time it multiple times so you can see how long the presentation really lasts. This will allow you to make changes and emphasize certain points longer than others, and build in your group exercises and activities if you have them. If you choose to practice silently, you will get through your presentation quicker than you really will and you may end up with a presentation that is too long. Typically, people speak faster during the actual presentation as they are nervous so it speeds up a little.

If you are going to practice then why not get some feedback before the actual big day. **Practice in front of a group,** a mirror and video tape yourself! If you are uncomfortable speaking in front of people, get your jitters out on friends or co-workers (or even your family). Never use your actual audience as the genie pig.

During your practice times, you can **modify your presentation as needed.** You may want to move some slides around or you may want to delete a few because you feel like you are being too repetitive with the same information. As the old saying goes, "Practice doesn't make perfection. Perfect practice makes perfect."

17 Steps to Delivery an Engaging Presentation

There are specific delivery steps you want to practice. After the presentation outline and manuscript are competed, many people don't know how to present the content or material in a way that will keep the audience engaged, support their learning styles, and help them to retain your information. These steps will guide you on how to present your material properly while achieving your goal of excellence.

The presentation outline parts will be included in these delivery steps to help you understand where the content you created gets included in the delivery of your presentation.

-----------------INTRODUCTION-----------------

Delivery Step 1: First Impression

Presentation Outline Parts:

Part 1: Welcome   **Part 2: Opening Statement**

Everything we have discussed will help to support delivering a great first impression to your audience: your dress, smile, posture, energy level, and your first words.

In the delivery step 1 of *First Impression*, you will include Part 1 the welcome after you enter the stage. You will transition from your welcome into Part 2 your strong opening statement that will set the stage for your presentation and will capture their attention within 90 seconds.

Delivery Step 2: Set a clear goal & explain why

Presentation Outline Part:

Part 3: Overall Goal

Step 2 is where you complete Part 3 of your overall goal for the audience. In this step you will set expectations for what the audience will be accountable for learning. You also want to explain "why" as that is important to gain buy in along with WIIFM which can motivate them to do the right behavior.

The best way to do this is by saying "My goal is [state the goal], so that [state the benefit]."

For example: My goal is that you gain confidence in public speaking, so that you can communicate effectively in any size group, live stream training, and reach your professional goals.

-----------BODY OF PRESENTATION-----------

Delivery Step 3: Share Agenda

Presentation Outline Part:

Part 4: Three Main Objectives

Share Part 4 the three main objectives with a few bullet points of what they will learn in these objectives. You share this in an agenda format so you can set clear expectations of what the audience should expect to learn.

Delivery Step 4: Objective #1 + Key Points + Evidence

Presentation Outline Parts:

Part 5: Key Points / Evidence

Now the stage is set, agenda is clear, and the audience is ready to learn. In delivery step 4 you begin to share the key points, and the evidence to support the first objective. You should have all this material completed in your manuscript and written in paragraph form.

Delivery Step 5: Ask Questions

You want to ask questions throughout your presentation so you can measure the group's retention of what you are teaching, and see if they are still awake and interested in what you are saying.

You can measure your pace by the audience's reaction. If they cannot answer your question, then you may need to slow down and review a few of your key points. If they are quick to answer, then you can keep moving forward.

Another reason you want to answer questions is a question can be used to clarify points you just covered with the group.

Asking questions is easy to do in a smaller live group presentation and little trickier on live stream. You can ask questions to the audience but be sure you read some of the answers from your audience to provide closure for the question so you can move on.

Delivery Step 6: Repeat Questions & Answers (Q & A's)

Anytime someone from a live audience asks a question, you want to repeat the question they are asking. You don't have to ask it exactly the way they did, you don't want it to sound like you are imitating them, so you can paraphrase it. You want to do this so you can ensure the rest of the group heard the question. This can prevent from receiving the same question multiple times.

Secondly, you want to repeat the question to clarify you heard the question correctly. You do not want to waste the group's time by answering the wrong question.

Also, if you are the one asking the questions to an audience member, then be sure and repeat their answer so the entire crowd knows what they said. It will keep them engaged, and they won't get a frustrating feeling that they don't know what is going on around them. It keeps a large group on the same page.

Delivery Step 7: Use Names First

When you are presenting to a live group with less than 60 people and they have nametags or nameplates, then you can call on them throughout the presentation. This is a great tactic to help to keep them on their toes because they don't know when their name will be called.

It makes training more personal & will grab their attention versus throwing out a question to the group. When you toss a question out to the entire group they usually don't answer because they are waiting on someone else to answer it or they are afraid to participate.

After you have called on multiple people throughout the presentation, the majority of the group wants to participate in the discussion and become more active.

Delivery Step 8: Activity / Role Play

Presentation Outline Parts:

Part 6: Activity / Role Play

You should not include an activity or role play after each main objective. You will probably only include one activity unless you are conducting a workshop that is hours long. The longer the training session the more hands-on the audience needs to be with activities and role-plays.

Delivery Step 9: Objective #2 + Key Points + Evidence

Presentation Outline Parts:

Part 5: Key Points / Evidence

Now you are getting into a routine. Just like you went through teaching the first objective, you will do the same for the other objectives.

Delivery Step 10: Complete Steps 5 – 8 while teaching Objective #2

Delivery Step 11: Review Material

In the outline you created, there are three main objectives with specific key points to support each. The best thing for the audience is to teach one of the objectives along with the key points, and then review before introducing the second objective. This helps the audience to keep up with your thoughts and to remember the material when you break it up into smaller portions.

The more repetition of the important information the better the audience will retain. It takes 7 times or more for a person to hear new information just to commit it to their short-term memory.

Delivery Step 12: Objective #3 + Key Points + Evidence

Presentation Outline Parts:

Part 5: Key Points / Evidence

Repeat the same format as you did for the two previous objectives.

Delivery Step 13: Complete Steps 5 – 8 while teaching Objective #3

-------------------CONCLUSION------------------

Delivery Step 14: Call to Action

Presentation Outline Parts:

Part 7: Call to Action

Now that you have taught all the material you want to include those action steps to ensure the audience understands what to do with the information you just taught.

Delivery Step 15: Review Objectives

Presentation Outline Parts:

Part 8: Review Objectives

Refer back to your presentation outline and review the main objectives. You can change how you present this by changing the verbiage of the agenda in Delivery Step 3. In the agenda slide you say, "Today we will cover…". On the review slide, you review the same objectives and bullet points on the agenda but you say, "Today, you learned…"

Delivery Step 16: Answering Questions

If there wasn't any time during the presentation to accept questions, then you may want to include this at the end of your presentation. When you are accepting questions from the audience there is a particular way you should respond to them.

Anytime someone from the audience asks a question, you want to repeat the question they are asking. You don't have to ask it exactly the way they did, you don't it to sound like you are imitating them, but you can paraphrase it. You want to do this so you can ensure the rest of the group heard the question. This can prevent from receiving the same question multiple times.

Secondly, you want to repeat the question to clarify you heard the question correctly. You do not want to waste the group's time by answering the wrong question.

Delivery Step 17: Bringing to a Close

Presentation Outline Parts:

Part 9: Closing Statement

Refer to Part 9 of your presentation outline, and be sure you tie this in with your strong opening statement and do not include any information. After you completed your closing statement, then you will need to exit the stage. You can end on a positive note by saying 'thank you' and encouraging them to join you on your favorite social media network to gain more knowledge or you can share your website with them.

Delivery Steps Diagram

If you are overwhelmed by the seventeen steps then don't be scared. Many of these steps are getting completed multiple times. Let me show you in a simple diagram.

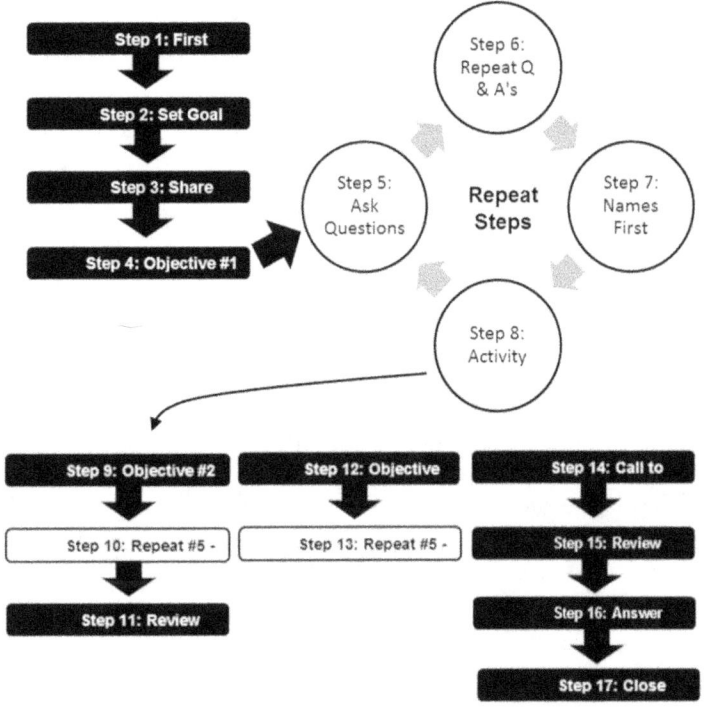

Self-Assessment

We can be harder on ourselves than other people so I wanted to include a self-assessment you can use to help develop yourself into a stronger public speaker. You can also use this assessment when practicing in front of a group, and they can answer these questions after you do a test run.

Instructions: Circle your response to each statement.

1. When I am speaking, I make direct eye contact with the majority of the audience members.

    strongly agree   agree   disagree   strongly disagree

2. I enjoy giving a speech or presentation to a group of people.

    strongly agree   agree   disagree   strongly disagree

3. When I give a presentation, I am able to hold everyone's attention and keep them engaged the entire time.

    strongly agree   agree   disagree   strongly disagree

4. I use hand gestures, facial expressions, and body language effectively.

    strongly agree   agree   disagree   strongly disagree

5. I keep my audience engaged by telling stories, asking questions, and planning applicable activities or role-plays.

    strongly agree   agree   disagree   strongly disagree

6. I am able to identify the main points and supporting details in an oral presentation and record them clearly in my notes.

strongly agree   agree   disagree   strongly disagree

7. After teaching multiple key points, I take the time to review.

strongly agree   agree   disagree   strongly disagree

8. My strongest skill as a speaker is _____.

9. One thing I can do to improve my listening skills is

_____.

10. On a scale of 1 – 10 with 10 being the best, how would you rank my overall presentation skills? _____.

Keep the Presentation Moving

Maintaining a high level of intensity and keeping the presentation moving for a long training session can be difficult.

Many tips such as **varying your style every 20 minutes**, having audience participation, etc. will help as well. However, how do you maintain the passion if you are running a half- or all-day session? A few pointers:

Schedule properly: Ensure you have adequate time for breaks. If the group is over 100 people, 15 minutes at a minimum is an absolute must. When the groups push 300+, 20 minutes is the minimum, especially if refreshments are served. Build these times into the agenda.

Follow the schedule: Start on time, end on time, and begin again on time. Manage the clock and use a break timer on the screen so people know when the break is over. Start immediately so the group gets the message from the outset!

Schedule informal interaction: Build 5-10 minutes into the beginning of a presentation right after lunch or a break to discuss what the group has liked so far or to answer any questions they may have. A more casual informal setting often encourages the questions to be asked.

PM slow down: After lunch is the dreaded spot. Therefore, when building your schedule, use this slot for team-building or upbeat, energetic type presentations (such as rapid roundtables or role playing) instead of 'another speaker' and a 'Data Dump'. You will need to get the audience moving or they may slip into a food coma.

Handling Questions & Objections

One area you need to be prepared for is to handle audience questions. Now even though you can't practice a group actually asking you questions, you can prepare yourself with possible questions and objections along with your proper response. There are different ways to get the audience's questions.

Most sessions allow for the audience to ask questions so think of some non-traditional ways to get this information in advance to better helping you answer the questions during your presentation. For example, when talking to or emailing participants about the session, ask what questions they have now. That way, you can build the answers into your presentation! If you have access to their email, the best way to gather feedback and questions is a survey. Survey Monkey is easy to use and it will analyze all your data which will save you a lot time.

Secondly, ask the group to write a list of questions at the beginning of the session. Then you want to instruct the group to check off the questions you have answered during the presentation. This way you can answer only the questions that didn't get answered during your presentation.

Another way of learning what the audience may want to learn is to kick off the meeting having each person or a few volunteers answer this question, "What do you expect to gain from today's presentation?" This will tell you what type of information you may need to highlight and it lets the entire group know you will be covering that during the speech. This is a great tactic but can only be used in small groups. However, you can ask this question on a live stream training and the participants can place their answers in live chat. As the presenter you can read off about five of the answers and then move into your opening statement.

The last way is to allow "off the cuff" questions after your presentation. You just need to be prepared to answer anything the audience may ask you.

When you are preparing your audience to ask questions, always phrase it as "What questions do you have?" instead of "Are there any questions?" When you phrase it this way it tells the audience that you want them to ask you questions and that you are expecting them to ask versus the second way which causes the audience to hesitant.

After you ask them "What questions do you have?" be sure to pause and remain comfortable with the silence. It may take some of them a little bit to come up with a question or to build up the nerve to ask in front of a big group. If the group is having a difficult time coming up with a question and you want to help get them started, then just say, "While you are coming up with your questions, one of the most popular questions I get asked is…"

On live stream, answering questions is a lot easier. With the live chat the audience will be sending in their questions throughout the entire presentation. When you are ready to answer questions, just have a member of your staff feed them to you.

When a question is finally asked always repeat the question especially in a large room to clarify it and ensure everyone heard the question. Before you give an answer, think through your answer. You want to be sure you don't act defensive. Since you will be on a time limit, don't waste time on irrelevant questions. In smaller groups you can discuss the answer one on one at the break or let them know you can discuss it "off-line" after the presentation. If it is in a larger group setting, then give a quick answer and then direct them down the area that you feel is more important.

Room Preparation

You can be in control of how you prepare yourself yet some things may feel out of your control and this can cause you to become nervous. Yet you can still follow up on some details to keep yourself calm and ensure everything is set and ready for your presentation. If you are not in 'control' of setting up the room then contact the meeting planner or person in charge of setup for the meeting to ensure you know what type of setup you will be dealing with. Remember to always get there early if you can to check out the room and follow up with the meeting planner.

Now at times, you can control the setup of the room and equipment so you want to ensure you address the following before the seminar:

1. **Room setup** – How will you setup the room to maximize the effectiveness of the type of presentation you are giving?

2. **'Feel' of the room.** What do you want the first impression to be when the audience enters? How will you engage all their senses? Sight, hear, taste, touch and smell? Pick some appropriate music to set the tone. Have the music running over a slide show of company or group photos or motivational quotes (available online at many websites).

3. **Equipment set up properly?** Ensure you know what type of A/V you will have so you can tailor your presentation around that; arrive early to practice and then set up the room to 'brand' your training. Always test the speakers and microphones and remember to have backups ready and tested also.

4. **Lighting of the room.** Learn how to adjust the lighting in the room so it is not too dark/light. Can you see the slides on the screen? Are you showing a video and need the lights dimmed during a particular time during your presentation? Who will help you do this and be sure to show them the correct lighting levels for before the video, during, and after.

Handling Things that Go Wrong

Rehearsal is a great form of practice and planning so rehearse 'mistakes' or when things go wrong. As the old saying goes, 'proper planning prevents poor performance.' Do you have a plan for the A/V (such as laptop, remote mouse, microphone or LCD) not working? What are you going to do if your live stream loses a signal? What will do you do if you an audio problems?

Sometimes there is information that may get skipped or is missing. Remember, only you know this so don't tattle on yourself and tell your participants. **Don't apologize** or even bring it up. Your audience will feel like they are missing out on something if you do this. Otherwise, they have no idea!

Always bring a **backup of your presentation** to load on another PC. Have a 2nd mouse and/or extra batteries.

Practice making mistakes such as the remote mouse not working. For example, if you do have a second mouse and the first stops working, be prepared with a group activity or poll of the audience to distract them and give you time to quickly replace the mouse w/your backup. If a microphone goes out, act like you are screaming or using large hand gestures to ease the discomfort and create a laugh (or have a hyperlink on every slide of your presentation w/a quote show or funny slide to buy you some time to address the issue). Seamless and effective!

If the issue **cannot be fixed immediately** (i.e. the microphone is out and you have no backup), have the audience take a short break or have a longer planned exercise or group activity to ensure enough time to fix the issue.

Chapter 7
Google Hangout on Air

> *Imagination is the beginning of*
> *creation. You imagine what you*
> *desire, you will what you imagine, and*
> *at last you will create what you will.*
> *~George Bernard Shaw*

What's a Hangout?

Hangout is a killer app for Google+'s. Hangout allows up to 10 people to "hang out" together in a shared space. You are able to speak to each other and see each other during the Hangout. Hangouts are easy to start, and it's easy to invite a group of people for a training session, brainstorming, or to just chat. Hangout allows people to screen share documents, switch audio/video devices, and connect from desktop or even mobile devices.

As we have been teaching in this book, you need to practice before you present to an audience, the same goes for Hangout but there is an additional step you must take. Before you try starting a Hangout on Air, you need to attend one. This way you can experience it from a participant standpoint. During this time you can write notes about what you liked and what you didn't like. Then you can apply those notes to your hangout. After you have attended a hangout, then host a few hangouts with some friends and test out all the features. You don't want to be fumbling during a presentation.

And so, What's a Hangout on Air? Hangouts on Air is a service from Google+ that lets up to 10 viewers watch your Hangout - within Google+ itself or live on YouTube. In fact, the video can be embedded into any website, so your viewers can literally watch it anywhere. You can broadcast for up to eight hours.

And after your broadcast, the final video version of the Hangout is uploaded automatically to YouTube for archive. People who missed the original broadcast can watch it after the fact.

Just imagine what's possible. You could replicate almost any existing television broadcast using Hangouts on Air technology. Reporters could be interviewing people in the middle of a protest. You could interview experts from across the world. There are no limitations with Hangout, only your imagination and willingness to overcome the fear of technical hurdles.

Getting Ready

You've got an idea for a show or training session, and you want to use the Hangout on Air to broadcast your idea to the world. Before you get started, there are a few steps you'll need to take.

Verify your YouTube Account

Before you do anything, make sure you have verified your YouTube account. You want to make sure your account can handle videos longer than 15 minutes, otherwise, your Hangout won't get saved. This is one of the most common mistakes people complain about. And unfortunately, if you fail to do this, your Hangout is probably gone forever. You don't want all your efforts to be wasted.

Equipment You'll Need

You can run a Hangout on Air with almost any laptop/tablet/phone, but you'll be seriously disappointed in the final result. You'll wish you'd invested in a better setup, for the host and the guests, to improve the production quality of the final video. There are so many factors that affect the quality of the video, so you want to start with the highest possible production quality.

- **Video Camera** - The quality of your webcam matters a lot. You'll want a webcam with HD resolution, low light sensitivity and good optics. A 1080p Logitech gets a lot of compliments. Whatever you do, don't settle for a cheap, crappy embedded webcams on a laptop - even Macbook cameras aren't good enough. You will look fuzzy and unprofessional.

- **Microphone** - Just as important as the camera, the quality of the microphone matters a tremendous amount. And the microphones on laptops are totally unacceptable. Again, even if a person claims their Macbook mic is pretty good... it's not. Spend a few bucks and get a separate USB device. There are a lot of different ones but I would avoid the headset as that is a lot of headgear. It looks more professional without wearing the headgear on the hangout.

- **Computer** - Run your Hangout on the fastest computer you can get your hands on. A low-end netbook isn't going to cut it. Do not start the Hangout from your tablet or phone. Use a laptop or a desktop computer with some horsepower. That will make sure the video is as smooth as possible.

- **Wired Internet Connection** - It's not always possible to get a hard-wired connection to the Internet. But if you can plug directly into a router, do that. Faster internet will give you smoother video.

- **Headphones** - One of the biggest problems with Hangouts is echo, where the audio from your speakers goes back into the computer microphone. There is nothing more distracting to the guests and the audience than echo in the broadcast. Google+ does have pretty great echo-cancelling technology, but it's not always perfect. You can require everyone on the Hangout to be wearing headphones, to minimize the risk of echo.

The Software to Use

Just as important as your equipment is the software you're running on your computer. Fortunately, you can start Hangouts on Air from any major operating system.

- **Browser** - Use Google Chrome. Seriously, Google makes Google+, and they make Chrome. The two were meant to go together, and that's where the majority of testing has happened. When people are having trouble with the tech, it is usually because they're using Safari or Firefox. Just use Chrome. That said, you might want to keep another modern browser on your computer. If you're having a problem with Chrome, try another as a backup.

- **Google Talk Plugin** - When you first try to join a Hangout, Google will walk you through installing the Google Talk Plugin. Why wait? Go ahead and install it right now.

- **Minimize Your System** - Before you start up a Hangout on Air, go ahead and reboot your computer. Then close every extraneous program that you won't need while you're running your Hangout. These can be intrusive and pop-up during a broadcast, or force your computer to scan for viruses when it really should be broadcasting a show.

- **Minimize Your Browser** - Depending on the show, you might want to screen share your browser to the audience. Remove all the extra toolbars and bookmarks from your browser. That'll give you more screen real estate and minimize the risk that you'll accidentally share something personal. It's even safer to run an Incognito window as your sharing browser, since it won't load any of your Chrome plugins and minimize the risk of browser fail.

Setting Up Your Office

Here are some simple things that you can do to provide the highest quality backdrop you can.

- **Avoid Backlighting** - The worst thing you can do is position yourself with a bright light or window to your back. The camera will try to set the brightness based on the bright background, and your face will be in shadow. Always get the bright windows shining on your face, with your back to a darker area of the house or office.

- **Illuminate Your Face** - In addition to removing any backlighting, you'll probably still want some kind of fill lighting for your face. A small desk lamp pointed at your face will probably do the trick, to make you pop off the background.

- **Have an Interesting Background** - A plain white wall is really boring, but a nice living room can look pretty great. Other people like to put a bookshelf behind them.

- **Position the Camera Above Your Eyes** - When you use a laptop camera, it's looking up at you, right up your nose. Instead, you want the camera positioned above you, so you're looking up into the camera a little bit. Trust me, it's more flattering. Put your laptop on some books, or put the camera on a tripod if you can.

- **Reduce the External Sounds** - You'll want to chase down every source of external sound and remove it. Turn off the ringer on your cell phone and beg the kids to be quiet (hah, good luck),

Before you go Live...

You've got your equipment tested and ready to go, you've convinced all your participants to show up at the right time, and you've turned the ringer off on your cell phone. You're ready to go live.

But wait, there are a few things you need to do first.

Create an Event for Your Hangout on Air

Several days before your broadcast, you'll want to create an Event in Google+. This will let people know your broadcast is happening, but also give you a permanent place to direct people beforehand. Anyone who shows up at the page can click "Yes" they'll be attending, and the Hangout on Air will get placed into their Google Calendar. That's a huge marketing benefit, since people will forget to tune in.

This is important; make sure you set your Event as a Public event and not a Hangout. I repeat, do NOT select Hangout for your Event, since that will mean a regular Google+ Hangout, and your viewers will end up in a Hangout with each other, wondering where you are.

Creating an Event is probably the single most important step you can make for marketing your Hangout on Air, as it serves as the backbone of your entire broadcast, and gives people a permanent location to jump off from.

The second important point is to include a unique #hashtag in your Event description, down at the end. For example, if we're recording Episode 50 of Presentation for Dummies, I'll include #PFD50 down at the end of the Event description. This will help you search and find your Event in the future.

Organize a Circle for the Group

Next up, you need to get everyone in circles. Create a Circle in Google+ for this Hangout and put all the participants into it. For example, if you were going to have an interview with the cast of *Star Wars*, create a new Circle called **Star Wars Hangout** and then circle Mark Hamill, Carrie Fisher, etc. You'll also want to include any other members of your team who might want to join the broadcast or help produce it.

Then share out the Circle to all the members in the circle and encourage them to import that Circle as well. You want everyone to be in everyone else's Circles.

This is important because when the Hangout starts, your participants might have a tough time figuring out where they're supposed to be. You'll try to +mention them to get them into the Hangout, but you haven't got them in a circle, so it's almost impossible to figure out the correct John Smith from all the others.

Make sure you haven't accidentally blocked any of the participants, and they haven't blocked each other. That'll prevent them from joining the Hangout.

Alternative Communication Lines

If your guests are having a tough time getting into the Hangout (*and they will*), you'll want to set up an alternative line of communication, so you can reach people. Create a contact list in your email program so you can send an email blast out to everyone.

For example, if a person is having trouble getting into the Hangout, you can email them the URL once the Hangout has started, but before you go live on air. Anyone who clicks that link is automatically brought into the Hangout. To be able to do this you need to have this set up in advance.

Create Your Hangout Graphics

To improve the production quality of your Hangouts, you'll want to create some graphics in advance. At the bare minimum, you'll want to make a starter screen, something you can put up at the very beginning to let people know the Hangout is about to start.

Going Live

You've done all your preparations, there's nothing left but to start your broadcast and put on a show. Don't worry, nothing will happen until you actually choose to go live. You can still turn back...

Initializing a Hangout on Air

If this is your first time, I highly recommend your start up your Hangout at least 30 minutes before the point you're expected to start broadcasting. This will give you time to chase down all the participants, make sure their gear is working properly, and they've had a chance to get comfortable with the technology (and bored of playing with all the toys).

You can access the Hangouts on Air functionality from the left menu in Google+. You should see a yellow icon that says "Hangouts on Air". This is where you'd normally go to watch a Hangout, but you can also start them from here.

In the upper right-hand corner of this page, there's a button that says. "Start a Hangout on Air". Okay, click that.

Next you'll be asked to give your Hangout a name, and you can invite the attendees who will be in the broadcast. Now you can just type in the circle name, and the Hangout will automatically invite all those people. You can also put in email addresses if you're having trouble inviting specific people.

Important, there's no way to invite the Public into a Hangout on Air (that would be chaos). Then click "Start a Hangout on Air".

Don't worry, you're not actually broadcasting... yet.

Welcome to the Green Room

Before you actually broadcast your Hangout on Air, Google+ puts you and the other participants into a Green Room version of your Hangout. You can all talk to each other and get prepared, but nobody in your audience can see you until the host actually clicks "Start Broadcast". Again, this gives you time to get things organized, work through technical issues, and chase down participants.

As the host, you've got a bunch of tasks you've got to do:

- **Install the Hangout Toolbox** - You and every participant in the Hangout will need to install the Hangout Toolbox app. This gives you the Lower Third and helps you keep track of comments. To install the plugin, click on "View More Apps" on the lower left-hand side of the Hangout. Then search for Hangout Toolbox. Once one person has installed it, everyone else in the Hangout will see it in their menu and can install it easily.

- **Embed the Live Stream Back into the Event Page** - This is tricky, but super important. Click the "Embed" button at the top of the Hangout to access your YouTube embed code. You'll copy-paste the youtu.be short URL and then paste it back into your Event page, so viewers can watch it right there. Click Edit Event -> Advanced -> Show All Fields. Copy-paste the URL into the YouTube field.

- **Embed the Live Stream Anywhere You Want** - After you've embedded the youtu.be link in the Event, go ahead and embed the video in any other places you want people to watch it. Your own website, for example.

- **Configure the Comments in Hangout Toolbox** - When you start broadcasting, the public is going to be trying to interact with you - in many different locations: YouTube, Twitter, Google+, your Event Page, etc. You'll want to read a more detailed tutorial on using Hangout Toolbox comments. But essentially, click on the green comments icon from within the Hangout Toolbox app, and then add sources. The YouTube source is added automatically, but you'll want to add any Twitter hashtags, or Google+ pages. Remember when you made that unique #hashtag? Search for it here and you'll be able to add the Event page to your list of sources.

- **Hide All the Participants** - You're just about to go live, so mute the video of all the participants except for the host. Hold your mouse over each user and you'll see a little button that lets you Hide From Broadcast. You'll bring everyone back shortly. Remind them that they've got to unmute themselves during the broadcast.

- **Put Up Your Opening Screen** - Use the screen share functionality of Hangouts on Air to put up an opening screen. Something that tells your audience that the broadcast is about to start. You'll have this up for the first 5 minutes or so, to get everyone watching the Hangout.

- **You want to kick someone off the Hangout**? You can do this by placing the mouse over their profile photo and click 'eject'.

Start Your Broadcast

The participants are hidden; your opening screen is up. Go ahead and click "Start Broadcast". You'll see a countdown, and then the "On Air" button will light up. This means your hangout is now live to the public. Until you click "End Broadcast", everything you do will be visible, so act accordingly.

We typically keep the starting screen up for about 5 minutes. This gives us time to further promote that the Hangout is happening, and give the public a chance to settle down. You'll see the number of viewers rise and rise.

And then, when you're ready:

- **Remove the Starting Screen** - Just click 'screenshare' and it'll disappear.

- **Bring the Hidden Participants Back** - Hold your mouse over each participant and then click "Show in Broadcast", and they'll appear to the public.

Running a Hangout on Air

I'm not sure what you had in mind, but I'm assuming some kind of show. You'll have a host/moderator, and then guests who will take turns talking.

But seriously, let your imagination flow. Consider what's possible with a mixture of devices, with people actually on location reporting on breaking news. You could perform a play, or show a behind the scenes broadcast from some event or show.

How long you let it run, who participates and how is all up to you. Make something cool.

It's okay to be casual and make mistakes. Viewers appreciate that it's real and they're not seeing some overly slick production. But try to create the highest production quality you can.

Important: A Hangout on Air is limited to a maximum of 8 hours (at the time this book was published).

Directing What Gets Broadcast

As the person who set up the Hangout on Air, you're in control of the camera. You can decide what gets seen by the public, and what is hidden.

If you don't do anything, the Hangout on Air will default to audio control. The main camera will switch to whoever's talking, and the audience will see that as well. If you're talking, the camera's on you, and then if someone interrupts, the camera will switch to them. In fact, if someone coughs during the broadcast, the camera will switch to them.

Instead of letting the Hangout control, you can click on individual people in the Filmstrip and lock the camera on them. Even if someone else is talking, the audience will see this person larger in the broadcast.

Important: Don't forget to switch. A common mistake is to leave the camera focused on the wrong person.

Interacting with the Guests

You're going to be running a show, so you'll be busy. But if you want to interact with the guests in a way that the audience can't see, you can use the Chat window. Click "Chat" in the upper left-hand corner of the Hangout Screen. The audience can't see the contents of the chat.

Muting, Hiding and Ejecting

As the host, you have total control over who's in the Hangout.

- **Mute Audio** - You can mute participants at any time, shutting their audio out of the broadcast. Just hold your mouse over their video in the Film Strip and then click the mute button. In fact, anyone in the Hangout can do this. Yet only the participant can unmute themselves again.

- **Hide/Show in Broadcast** - If you need to hide a person from the broadcast, hold your mouse over them and click "Hide from Broadcast". Then you can bring them back again with "Show in Broadcast". If people enter your Hangout on Air after it's started, they'll automatically be hidden, so you'll need to Show them to the audience. After a person has been hidden, they'll need to unmute their own audio.

- **Eject a Participant** - As the host of the event, you can also kick anyone out of the broadcast. This isn't necessarily because they're being a jerk; although, that's a great reason to kick someone. We also use this to free up space in a big Hangout to bring in another guest. Make sure you don't Block the person (unless they're a jerk, then go ahead and block them so they'll never come into another Hangout with you).

Screensharing

At various points in the broadcast you or the participants might want to display an image or video to the public. As the host, you can switch camera focus onto this, even while someone else is talking.

As the host, you can select the participant for the main screen and keep the image up, even if another participant is talking. It only takes a second to download an image and then screen share it to enhance the broadcast.

- **Respect Copyright** - Many of the images or videos you'll want to use will be owned by someone else. Familiarize yourself with fair use laws, or get permission for any images you're planning to use in your broadcast. The best method is to just create your own images.

- **No Audio with Videos** - You can screen share a video, either with your local video player or YouTube, but there's no way to share the audio. If you really want the audio, you'll need to create a loopback, where you take the audio from your speakers and route it back through your microphone.

- **Share the Load** - Encourage other members of the Hangout to find and screen share appropriate images whenever possible. As the host, you'll notice the images and switch over to make them prominent in the broadcast.

Interacting with the Audience

A Hangout on Air is live, so you can absolutely interact with the audience. But it's pretty complicated for the people watching your show to know where to post their comments, and it's even harder for you to see where the comments are being made.

The Hangout Toolbox Comment Tracker is absolutely essential for this. It will scoop up comments from a variety of sources and then display them in a single thread within the Hangout.

- **Have You Got All the Sources?** - Hangout Toolbox Comment Tracker lets you track multiple sources at the same time. From your Event, the Google+ profile that hosts the Hangout on Air, Twitter, YouTube, and searches on Google+. Make sure you get them all, so that people aren't asking questions you'll never see.

- **Announce How Viewers Can Comment** - Early on in the broadcast, explain to your viewers how they can chat with you. Tell them they can comment on the Event Page, in YouTube, on Twitter using a #hashtag, etc.

- **Engage Your Viewers** – Your viewers will enjoy the Hangout more if you get them involved by answering questions and post their images in the Hangout.

- **Get Everyone to Interact with Viewers** - As the host, you'll be busy. So encourage the rest of the panel to interact with viewers in the chat, on Twitter, YouTube, the Event page, etc. Get them to post links to relevant sources and answer questions that viewers might have. Many hands make light work.

After the Hangout

When you're done with your show, click "End Broadcast". That will wrap up your show and archive it on YouTube. The viewers will no longer be able to see the contents of the Hangout. However, the members of the Hangout will still be able to see each other and interact. We'll often stick around after a broadcast for a few minutes to discuss what we did well and what we need to change for the next one.

Encourage your attendee to help you promote the final archived video.

If you want to you can edit the final video; either use the built-in tools from YouTube to trim and annotate your video, or download the video and edit it with a professional video editor. You can't replace the existing video, unfortunately.

Now that the final video is out there for the world to see, be sure you do your best to market the video and get the most from your efforts.

Final Conclusion

Public speaking is something that you can master at any level: on stage, video streaming, Hangout, or small group facilitation. All the steps given in this book will help you to write and execute a captivating presentation every time.

Remember to prepare your content, practice for perfection, and have fun during the presentation.

ABOUT THE AUTHOR

Cheryl Stinchcomb has 20+ years in the training industry as a leadership trainer, training program developer, and speaker. She has written materials and/or personally trained for these prominent companies such as:

- The Walt Disney Company
- Kentucky Fried Chicken (KFC)
- Red Robin Gourmet Burgers
- 7-Eleven, Inc.
- Pizza Hut International
- Outback Steakhouse
- Council for Hotel & Restaurant Trainers
- Tropical Smoothie Cafe
- Camille's Sidewalk Cafe
- Los Cabos Mexican Grill & Cantina
- Waterfront Grill

Cheryl is also the author of *Pinterest for Profits, How to Master Pinterest in 15 Days* and the creator of *Profit Pinning*, an online course that teaches business owners how to master Pinterest Marketing in a 25-day video challenge.

www.ingramcontent.com/pod-product-compliance
Lightning Source LLC
Chambersburg PA
CBHW051313170526
45166CB00002B/532

* 9 7 8 1 5 0 0 1 8 1 1 0 9 *